N MORE TENKO

MY WAR – LIFE AS A JAPANESE PRISONER
OF WAR 1942-45

BUILDING THE CENTRAL SUMATRA RAILWAY
PEKANBARU TO MUARO 1944–45.

By
W R Smith
Co Author J N Walker

Grosvenor House
Publishing Limited

This book is published by
Grosvenor House Publishing Ltd
Link House
140 The Broadway, Tolworth, Surrey, KT6 7HT.
www.grosvenorhousepublishing.co.uk

A CIP record for this book
is available from the British Library

ISBN 978-1-78623-068-3

To my late parents
Walter and Gertrude Smith
who, with great fortitude,
waited fifteen months without
any news, beyond 'posted missing'.

CONTENTS

Introduction

Walter Raymond (Ray) Smith was born in Penrith, Cumberland, a small market town in the North West of England. He was educated in the town and on leaving school was apprenticed to G & J Thompson a local agricultural engineering firm.

When war with Germany was declared in September 1939 he was only 16 years old but, like a lot of young men of his age, he held a strong desire to serve his country in its time of need. He nurtured this thought for some time and in May 1940, even though he was still only 17 (and under age), he sought the approval of his parents to 'join up'. They reluctantly agreed and by declaring his age as 18 he enlisted with the RAF and trained as an Armourer to become Aircraftsman 1st Class 1005445 Smith W R.

In June 1941 he left Britain for the Far East arriving first in Singapore, then Malaya (now Malaysia) and finally in Java, Indonesia (the former Dutch East Indies). He saw little action as, shortly after their attack on Pearl Harbour on 7 December 1941, the Japanese invaded Java and quickly overran the Allied Forces.

Ray was captured on 8 March 1942 at Tasikmalaya on Java and spent the rest of the war in captivity in Japanese POW camps. He was held in several camps, eventually transferring to Sumatra where he was involved in building the Trans Sumatra Railway (Pekanbaru to Muaro -137 miles). Having been captured at such a young age he felt that he had to make the best of what was on offer. He learnt to speak Dutch, Malay and basic Japanese and for the last 18 months of captivity was recognized as the Camp Interpreter. This gave rise to several interesting encounters.

In August 1945, when the Japanese finally surrendered, Ray was in such a remote location on Sumatra that it took weeks for him and his fellow prisoners to finally reach freedom. When he left home in May 1940 he asked his mother to promise that when he returned home she had to greet him as if he was simply returning from work. He finally reached home on 11 November 1945 and,yes, his mother was true to her word. He was only 1,616 days late. 1,294 of which had been spent in captivity.

The Commandant of Ray's last POW Camp was a compassionate man called Tadaiti Ebinuma who did his best to protect the POWs from the excesses of the Railway Engineers. After the Japanese surrender it was agreed that Ebinuma would be provided with a letter indicating his compassionate nature and willingness to help the POWs in the hope that should he ever appear before a war tribunal his conduct would be taken into account and, perhaps, influence any decision as to punishment. One of Ray's last tasks as Camp Interpreter was to write this letter. Ebinuma was sent to Changi Jail in Singapore and detained there until he appeared before the War Crimes Commission sitting in Singapore in May 1947. Like many other Camp Commandants he was expecting to be sentenced to death. The Commission felt that the time he had already spent in prison was sufficient punishment so he was released and returned to Japan. After his release he wrote to Ray thanking him for the letter saying that it may have saved his life. Ray's family and Ebinuma's family have since met. Ebinuma died in 1979 aged 76.

Ray married his childhood sweetheart Marie in 1946. They had 3 children. Susan born in 1949. Judith born in 1953 and Peter born in 1961. Marie sadly died in 1987 and Ray passed away in 2003. This is his account of his war time experience. It is entirely factual, humorous in parts, deadly serious in others but more than anything serves to remind us of the hardships and depravation endured by our brave young men to ensure that the freedom we all cherish so much continues to be enjoyed. His ability to recall names, dates and actual occurrences, which are described in precise detail, is outstanding and testimony to the man that he was.

CHAPTER ONE

Enlistment and Training

From 1939 to 1945 there was a war. It became known as The Second World War. The comedians of the time would say '*You should know about it. It's been in all the papers*'. It was a war that affected nearly every household in all the participating countries. Not least if it involved the loss of a loved one.

This is an account of 'My War'. OK there was Churchill, Eisenhower, Montgomery, Slim, Mc Arthur and Mountbatten but I didn't have much to do with them. Come to think of it they didn't have much to do with me either.

How well I remember the announcement made by Neville Chamberlain on Sunday 3 September 1939 that '*A state of war existed between Britain and Germany*'. At the ripe old age of 16 years and 5 months and living in a small market town called Penrith in the north of England it was difficult to imagine how this historical announcement was going to affect me. Conscription to HM Forces had been in operation for some time as the possibility of war with Germany seemed inevitable. This meant that several of my 'mates' had received their 'Call-Up' papers requiring them to report to a given place at a given time. This in turn had a negative impact on social activities as even the local Territorial Army members were 'called up' very early and soon found themselves in France fighting the enemy.

Black Outs, Food Rationing, Evacuation of Children from cities to the countryside and the almost continuous departure of young men into the armed forces were constant reminders of *'the state of war'* that existed even though the conflict had not yet reached British soil.

At this time I was employed as an apprentice in a local agricultural supply company and could possibly claim that this was a 'Reserved Occupation' allowing me to avoid conscription if necessary. As a complete contradiction I harboured this deep feeling of wanting to 'Join Up' by offering myself as a volunteer. By now it was May 1940 meaning that the war had been going on for some 8 months. I made my feelings known to my parents who reluctantly agreed and I opted for the Royal Air Force and visited the RAF Recruiting Office at Carlisle. By volunteering I felt that I had some leverage in asking for an Air Force trade of my choice and had set my sights on becoming an armourer. Otherwise I could abandon the whole idea as I was not compelled to join at all.

I was pleasantly surprised how everything seemed to fall into place. I had a medical there and then which I obviously passed as I was told to await my official 'Call Up'. I also established that I would train in my chosen trade. However, one important matter remained to be dealt with. The minimum age for enlistment was 18. I had achieved 17 years and 1 month and was surprised and quite relieved that I was never asked to provide proof of my age. This deceit about my age had two very important consequences. Firstly, that in the years that followed and subsequent events meant that my mother and father had bitter recriminations about giving their approval. Secondly, I was acutely aware that if my deceit ever came to light I could be 'drummed out' of the Service with ignominy. I will describe later how I avoided detection 'by the skin of my teeth'.

The OHMS Call Up letter subsequently arrived. I was required by no less than The King to report to the Recruiting Depot at Padgate near Warrington on 18 June 1940. Here the enlistment process began with great speed and vigour. On that particular day I was sworn in, kitted out, injected and vaccinated. When one of my contempories had the temerity to ask the Orderly Disciplinary Corporal about the apparent haste, he was told *'Look laddie we are needing 'em not feeding 'em'*. At the same time I recall receiving my Service Number which was printed on a slip of paper advising me that I was '1005445 Smith W R Aircraftsman 2nd Class under training as an Armourer (Guns)'. The last distinction wasn't immediately clear but was to become abundantly clear some weeks later.

Sleep did not come easily on the first night in Barracks. The efforts of the Medical Orderlies earlier in the day resulted in violent throbbing in both arms making it difficult to find a comfortable position. Tiredness eventually won and I slipped into deep sleep only to be awoken by the sound of Air Raid Sirens indicating an impending attack on nearby Liverpool. On the orders of the Corporal the Barrack room was evacuated in favour of the rather unwelcome Air Raid Shelter with its musty, damp smell. This was a completely new experience. The night was full moonlight and the drone of the German bombers sounded very near yet I was puzzled as to why I couldn't see them as they made their deadly attack.

The next two days involved basic drill on the 'Drill Square' otherwise known as 'The Sacred Acre'. The Corporal whose word and command were final took great delight in ridiculing the recruits and even though he was mentally inferior to many of them his position meant that he was never challenged. This was the first experience of drill and discipline to most of the recruits and on many occasions the Corporal's ridicule was justified as a fair number of recruits had great difficulty distinguishing *right* from *left*. So a simple command like *'Right Turn'* resulted in chaos and a torrent of abuse from the Corporal in a language that an innocent lad from Penrith had difficulty understanding. It illustrated perfectly the old Sergeant Major's response of *'You may have broken your mother's heart but you aren't going to break mine'*.

On 21 June we got our first taste of 'Unit Movement'. On day one, in addition to basic uniform, we were also issued with webbing harness, full back pack, side pack and large kit bag. Thankfully we were only going to the Disciplinary Training Centre (DTC) at Wilmslow in Cheshire. A relatively short journey as I wasn't looking forward to having to 'hump' all the bulky kit. The next 28 days were to be spent at the DTC on marching drill, firearms drill and physical training. This would culminate in a 'Passing Out Parade' in front of the Commanding Officer. Once again we were allocated a Discipline Corporal or 'Tin God' whose sole task was to knock us into shape in preparation for the Passing Out Parade. Short back and sides were the order of the day which meant a visit to the camp barber who provided only the standard 'Service' haircut despite several requests from the more tonsorial endowed to be left with their wavy adornments.

I mentioned earlier the anxiety caused by lying about my age and the fear of being detected. Well this is where I nearly came unstuck. At the DTC I received a message from the Wing Orderly Room to report to the Duty Flight Sergeant. This gentleman then directed me to 'Pay and Accounts' who told me that I hadn't handed in my Unemployment and Health Insurance cards. These were two distinctly separate cards and the stamps attached to them were of a specific colour which clearly denoted 'UNDER 18 YEARS'. As I left the building my problem became immediate. What could I do? I felt resigned to the fact that my short stay with the RAF was about to come to an end. I then went to the 'phone box and called Dad in his Office at Penrith. I explained the position to him and told him that he had no alternative than to post the Cards to me. Almost as an aside I asked him if there was anything he could do to resolve my predicament.

His reply '*I will see*' gave me some heart. But this was short lived as that night I reflected on my parents' position and felt that it was in their interests to restore me to Civilian life in a 'Reserved Occupation'. As good as his word Dad had sent me the Cards as a few days later I was asked to collect and sign for a registered packet from the Post Orderly. I opened it immediately to find two cards both showing my name and National Health Number and to my complete delight I saw that they were both in the colour indicating 'OVER 18'. It transpired that Dad had a close associate in the Unemployment Exchange who happened to have access to a set of cards which had been handed in as 'found' and with a little ingenuity was able to adapt them to appear as if they were mine. Easy when you have the right 'contacts'. My cards were never queried by Pay and Accounts.

Anyway, the training period had now come to an end resulting in the dreaded Passing Out Parade. I have to say that the ungainly squad of 'sproggs' that arrived on 21 June had miraculously transformed into a unit that gave a faultless display and a performance to be proud of. Even the Discipline Corporal was impressed and went to great lengths to explain that it was tradition for the squad to take him to the local hostelry and 'entertain' him. We reluctantly agreed and even though he was a figure we despised we also had a certain admiration for what he had allowed us to achieve.

On 22 July we were on the move yet again. This time by train to Hereford to the RAF College known as No 11 School of Technical Training (No 11 SofTT) which was located in a small village called Credenhill. To those in the know it rejoiced in the nickname Spratt's Concentration Camp derived from the Commanding Officer's name Group Captain Spratt. The SofTT had four barrack blocks (wings in RAF parlance). Discipline was strictly applied. You marched everywhere. Each wing had its own Military Band which accompanied you wherever you marched. Marching, accompanied by your Band even took place on a Saturday afternoon and on one occasion an airman was heard to remark '*You even need a band to take you to the ablutions*'.

Technical training took place in classrooms and was very intense. The aim was to achieve a pass in the Local Trade Test Board (LTTB) examination. All of my group

(Class 34) had to sit a lengthy written examination followed by four practical examinations conducted on a one to one basis. By way of speeding up the training for that of Armourer, the Trade had been split into Armourer (Guns) and Armourer (Bombs). The 'Bombs' training took place in East Anglia. Individual approaches to these examinations differed greatly. 1 Conscripts did not have the same enthusiasm to pass as Volunteers. 2 Those who had come from technical occupations in 'Civvy Street' found it difficult to adjust to the RAF way. 3 Teachers and those from a similar background in 'Civvy Street' found the written examinations quite easy but had difficulty applying this knowledge to practical situations. There were three pass levels for the examination. Aircraftsman 2nd Class – 40%. Aircraftsman 1st Class – 60%. Leading Aircraftsman – 80%. Results would be announced the day following the examination. A pass at any of the three levels carried with it a Railway Warrant and Home Leave. A fail carried no such reward and meant remaining in Camp with a promise (not always honoured) of re-entry on to a later Course.

When the results were announced I was rather dramatically called by my Tutor and told that I had achieved 59.9% and as I was so close to the 60% pass level I could re-sit the exam if I chose to. I had nothing to lose so I accepted the offer. On entering the exam room and to my surprise I knew the Invigilator. I was uneasy as I wasn't sure whether this was an advantage or a disadvantage. Anyway I passed and would soon be going home.

A very welcome home leave followed, meeting my parents for the first time since 'Joining Up'. I noticed that the return part of my railway warrant was to Bridgend in South Wales. This made sense as it was explained at Hereford that those achieving 60% or more would attend a 'Conversion Course' success on which would result in the Trade Designation 'Fitter Armourer'. (Those achieving less than 60% would be posted to Active Service Squadrons). The date for reporting to Bridgend was 6 December 1940. The Unit was known as Stormy Down and was situated on the south coast of Wales adjacent to the Bristol Channel. I duly reported as instructed only to be informed that the Unit was due to close in January 1941 and so it did on the 17th. So in less than six weeks I was on the move again. This time to No 8 SofTT based at RAF Weeton near Blackpool in Lancashire. I arrived at Kirkham Railway Station and we were transferred by road to Weeton Camp. It was dark on arrival and I remember seeing some figures returning to their billets through the snow and also recall one of them shouting *'Hard luck mates. Give us Dunkirk before this place any time'*.

I took some consolation in knowing that this posting was the closest to home since I enlisted.

Training was mostly of a practical nature as this was a Fitters Conversion Course and was aimed at providing the necessary knowledge and skills to pass practical tests towards the end of April. I achieved 45% in the tests and this was followed closely by a thorough Medical Examination the purpose of which puzzled me for some time as I had already had such an examination and as far as I was aware nothing had changed. Eventually it was leaked that this was to identify those who were suitable for Overseas Duty and those who weren't. Those suitable for an overseas posting would be posted to a Draft Centre. Just prior to the customary end of course leave we were all supplied with a form which we had to complete indicating our 1st and 2nd choices of RAF Stations that we wished to be posted to. This seemed too good to be true and indeed it was. I hopefully entered Silloth (some 20 miles from home) as my first choice. Aircraftsman Hartley who lived at Grangemouth in Scotland couldn't believe his luck. There was an RAF Station at Grangemouth so he obviously selected that as his first choice. As it turned out I was posted to Grangemouth and AC Hartley to Duxford in Cambridgeshire. Another 'Service' con!

Leave commenced on 29 April and I was to report to Grangemouth on 6 May. I duly reported and was billeted in a Junior School at Polmont near Falkirk. The Unit was No 58 Operational Training Unit (OTU) where would-be fighter pilots were trained on Spitfires and Hurricanes. Our job was to load the Browning Sub Machine Guns and Cine Cameras and to 'harmonise' the armaments to a common fighting range of 400 yards. In the armoury I was surprised to be re-united with the Corporal who conducted my LTTB test re-sit but he had been reduced in rank to Leading Aircraftsman for some misdemeanour which he was reluctant to discuss.

CHAPTER TWO

Off to War –The Journey to the Far East

On 6 June I was given 'Embarkation Leave' and told to return to Grangemouth on 10 June where I was to await further orders. These arrived on 13 June and I was told to report to the RAF Drafting Centre at West Kirkby in Cheshire. I travelled by train to the Drafting Centre and remained there until 28 June when under great secrecy and under armed guard (maybe they thought we were going to escape) we travelled by train to Liverpool Water Street Station. From there we were marched to the Pier Head then turned right along the quayside to the first vessel berthed at the quay. It was a Union Castle Passenger liner the MV Athlone Castle which had been converted into a troopship. We embarked and set sail in the early evening only to re-anchor midstream in the River Mersey. I felt a little uneasy as we could be a sitting target for the German Bombers who visited Liverpool almost nightly. Two other troopships were anchored alongside us making us an even bigger target. We eventually lifted anchor the following afternoon. Destination unknown!

We cleared the Formby Lightship and the more knowledgeable amongst us detected that we were turning almost directly onto a northern course. Speculation as to our destination was rife. The more optimistic suggested America. Off the River Clyde we joined a group of about ten other ships. One of these was a Polish ship which was much smaller than the rest. It was coal-fired and almost all of the time belched out clouds of black smoke. We formed a convoy of three rows of ships and were informed by our crew (Merchant Navy men) that convoy rules at sea meant that we would travel at the speed of the slowest ship which turned out to be the Polish one. We were warned that rubbish should never be thrown overboard as this would provide evidence of our presence to any lurking German 'U' boats. Lights were shaded during darkness and ship to ship messages were passed by Aldis Lamp in morse code as radio message were frequently inter-cepted by hostile vessels. For a number of days we sailed due westward in the North Atlantic easily ascertained by the sunrises and sunsets. Every hour on the hour all the ships regimentally changed course to follow a zig-zag pattern in order to confuse any hostile subma-rines. By now the Polish ship was no longer present. Had it been sunk or had it headed off on its own course? We then, as one, all made a sweeping left turn which meant that we were now travelling due south parallel to the American Seaboard. Day by day the weather became warmer and all the following bird life had disappeared. The conditions were now almost sub-tropical and another left turn (or should I say a turn to port) fol-lowed, which aroused more speculation as to our desti-nation. At the same time we were all required to attend the ship's sick bay to receive injections as 'boosters' to those given at West Kirkby. We had certain duties to perform on board, such as carrying crates of foodstuffs from the 'bowels' of the ship (E Deck) to the canteen at the stern of the ship (A Deck). We were entertained in the mess deck by concerts, housey-housey and the like and the Service Clergymen on the Draft held regular hymn singing sessions. Needless to say our favourite was *'Those in peril on the sea'*.

By now the constant drone of the propeller shafts below the cabin went unnoticed until it suddenly stopped. This meant that the engines had stopped. It was 2.30am. Curiosity got the better of most of us so we went up to the Promenade deck where, in the far distance, we could see land. At daybreak the engines restarted and we slowly moved towards the land. The crew revealed that ahead of us was Freetown, Sierra Leone in West Africa. It soon became clear why we had stopped out at sea. The entrance to Freetown harbour was protected by a submarine boom net which must remain closed during darkness to prevent access by a hostile submarine. As we edged slowly into the harbour we noticed a number of Native Bum Boats (I never did learn how they got that name) heading out towards us. We were told by the crew that they were 'money divers' who, if you threw coins into the water they would dive and return with the coin held firmly between their teeth. It was apparent that they had encountered visiting ships many times before as they would shout *'What about a Liverpool shilling?'* or *'Throw us a Glasgow tanner'*. Now and again a joker on board would throw something closely resembling a coin into the water and watch the diver disappear into the murky depths. On realising he had been duped his command of English swear words soon became apparent.

We remained in Freetown for three days then set sail turning to port heading for South Africa. Each day the weather became cooler and as we once again turned to an easterly direction we knew we were about to round the Cape of Good Hope. We soon encountered the notorious winds 'The Roaring Forties', an experience never to be forgotten. It is difficult to explain their severity without being accused of exaggeration. The huge ship was thrown about to most remarkable angles. The seas were mountainous. One minute it was possible to look down on the ship astern of us and the next minute to look right along the waterline. As the ship rolled from side to side I was convinced that at any moment we were about to 'turn turtle'. This pitching and rolling meant that quite often each of the twin propellers were clear of the water resulting in them revving up dramatically causing the whole ship to shudder and rattle. Not a pleasant experience. Sleeping was very difficult as you were tossed about in your bunk and any loose equipment crossed and re-crossed the floor at will. Naturally the incidence of seasickness increased during this time so the Mess Deck was much quieter than normal. This left a 'hard core' of those unaffected. I was one of them and visits to the Mess provided some interesting and amusing events. The floor in the mess deck was covered in shiny rubber tiles so to navigate the short distance from the servery to the fixed tables successfully was quite an achievement. As the ship lurched and tossed those less than competent diners quite frequently deposited their meal on the floor. This meant that the already slippery floor now resembled an ice rink. The sometimes cruel 'Service' humour meant that no warning was provided to an unsuspecting diner of the impending danger. Successful navigation was greeted by a loud applause and failure by a loud cheer. Eventually the winds subsided to the immense relief of everyone on board. We had survived and shortly afterwards sailed majestically into Durban harbour. South Africa was a country not at war. No blackouts, no rationing and as we were to find out most hospitable towards us. However, there was one amusing incident worth relating. From the top deck of our ship you could clearly see the roadway outside the dockyard. On the roadway was a throng of young ladies who were waving to us. They also repeatedly made an upwards motion with their right hands with the first and middle fingers prominently displayed. Now we all know that this has a less than complimentary meaning which was quite troubling. Not fully understanding this less than welcoming gesture we could see no problem with returning the compliment only to be told later that since leaving Liverpool, Winston Churchill had made his immortal speech culminating in his 'V' for Victory sign. So the ladies were simply repeating it as a welcome gesture. What a relief. We also noticed that most of the trucks, locomotives and cranes on the dockside had been daubed with the cipher …- which is Morse code for the letter V.

We remained in Durban for four days and were allowed shore leave for three of them. The locals were extremely kind and hospitable. As small groups of Servicemen came through the dock gates they would be met and taken off by car to be wined and dined and reminisce about life back in 'Blighty'. Opposite the docks was a Tattoo Parlour. Almost immediately a queue of would be clients formed. As they left the

Parlour I noticed that their 'artistry' was swollen and bleeding and covered simply by a piece of toilet paper. Hardly an incentive to have 'Mother' or 'Betty' or any other loved one immortalised on your body. Along with two colleagues I travelled by rickshaw into the City Centre. The driver was a six foot plus Zulu wearing tribal dress and headgear. He was barefoot and his lower legs were whitewashed to resemble white stockings. His muscular frame meant that he had no difficulty transporting three fully grown men and he was able to achieve a remarkable pace. At one point our speed was such that all three of us felt that we might tip over so at a pre-arranged signal we all leaned forward. This caused the driver to nearly lose his balance but it did have the effect of slowing him down. He showed his displeasure by shouting something in his native tongue which I presume were Zulu swear words.

An amusing event in Durban related to me and which is completely accurate involved an RAF Engine Fitter with the surname Litherland. He hailed from Liverpool. His parents had either a sense of humour or were completely devoid of imagination as they christened him Ferdinand. Ferdinand Litherland is quite a mouthful so in true service fashion this was shortened to Ferdie. He had some 'rough edges' but he was a likeable fellow with a magnetic personality. Whilst in Durban, Ferdie and two colleagues were approached by the wife and daughter of Durban's Head Postmaster and invited to dinner. The house was palatial with numerous black servants and staff. They were ushered into the very elegant dining room where aperitifs were served. Ferdie felt immediately at home and conveniently 'lost' his Scouse accent assuming *lad-de-dah* tones whilst he conversed with his guests. Everyone was about to take their seats around the dining table for the meal when Ferdie suddenly stood erect and said *'I'll tell you what, it isn't half hot in here'* then promptly picked up the finger bowl and quaffed its entire contents much to the amusement of all present.

On a more serious note this was our first experience of apartheid. Evidence of it was all around. Public benches, public transport, drinking establishments and the like all had clear lines of demarcation between 'Black' and 'White' which had to be strictly observed. Completely unfair and unreasonable to us newcomers. I patronised 'The Cumberland Bar' for obvious reasons. On one occasion we nearly caused a riot in the bar. We offered to buy the black barman a drink. Out of order for two reasons 1 He was black and 2 Treating was not allowed not even from white to white. (I never did understand why).

On our 5th day in Durban we were all required to parade on the Promenade Deck. This was for a 'head count' prior to setting sail. The effect of over imbibing whilst on shore leave soon became evident. Many of those on parade had to be wedged between colleagues to ensure that they remained stood up and the head count revealed that three servicemen had failed to make it so we set sail without them.

As soon as we had passed the three mile limit the ship's Captain opened his sealed Orders and passed them to the Senior Service Officers on board. Our destination was Singapore. There was much speculation on board ship that this would be our ultimate destination supported by the fact that we had been issued with tropical uniform.

As we sailed northward skirting Madagascar we were escorted by the heavy cruiser HMS Mauritius. One night after flashing a Morse message she turned full circle and set sail southward. We took this to mean that we were no longer in hostile waters. Our spare time was taken up in class learning elementary Malayan language. This absorbed me and interested me and as it turned out it would serve me well in the years to come.

We were in fact heading for Bombay (Mumbai) in India. On arriving in Bombay we tied up to a buoy in mid harbour to take on fuel, water and mail and shortly afterwards set sail for Colombo in Ceylon (now Sri Lanka). After taking on more provisions we set sail again and travelled down the Malacca Straits arriving at Keppel Harbour in Singapore on 25 August 1941. This harbour was to have significance in the lives of service personnel and civilians in times to come. We disembarked onto the quayside where a Regimental Band was playing. The heat was most oppressive, not helped by having to lug kitbags and packs and being dressed in full ceremonial khaki. We marched to the waiting motor transport and were quickly whisked away to a transit camp at Seletar which was a group of simple huts made out of bamboo and palm leaves. We were assured that our stay was only for one night. Next morning we paraded and were told to listen for our name and number and the new Unit to which we would be posted. Names such as Alor Star, Kuantan, Butterworth and Kuala Lumpur conjured up fascinating ideas. Mine was Kuala Lumpur (KL) which translates as Muddy River! I boarded the train for the journey to KL crossing the causeway that joins Singapore to Johore Bharu on the Malayan mainland and arrived at KL Railway Station which to this day is still a most impressive edifice. Not a bit like a railway station. From KL we travelled by motor transport on a short run to a place called Batu (stone) to my Unit (No 153 Maintenance Unit) which was new and purpose built. It was located amongst rubber, bamboo and palm trees which had been preserved during construction. The barrack rooms were randomly located rather than in the customary barrack lines. In the centre of the Unit was the NAAFI canteen, the hairdressers, the tailors and the cobblers. The floor level of the rooms was about 2'6" above ground, they were very airy and had mosquito nets (Klambus) arranged in rows and each room had four cooling fans suspended from the roof. Outside and attached to the building were the showers and washing facilities. Each billet had a 'Room Boy' who was required to clean the billet, store the Klambus, make the beds and manage the laundry. You could specify 'Lekas Dhobi' (Quick Laundry) which would be returned the same day. Our 'Room Boy' was an Indian Boy called Bishan Das. He was a lovely lad, quite shy but always wishing to please.

The Engine Repair Section (ERS) and General Engincering Section (GES) workshops were located on the same site as was the air conditioned Spare Parts Store. The camp was served by a short siding from the main North/South railway line so that aircraft engines and other mechanical appliances could be brought for scheduled maintenance and repairs although subsequent events meant that it never really got the opportunity to function properly. Even though the camp had an important and significant role to play the way it had been designed gave the impression of a holiday camp in a beautiful jungle setting.

Back in June 1940 when I was about to enlist in the RAF I was visited at my work place by a local chap called Bill Faulder. Bill was a very capable motor engineer employed by the West Cumberland Farmer's Trading Society. He was aware that I was about to enlist and told me that he had been 'called up' into the RAF and like me had to report to Padgate albeit a week earlier than me. My parting shot to him was 'We must look out for each other when we are there'. As I described earlier things moved very quickly at Padgate so I never did see him and even when I was on home leave I was often greeted by 'Bill Faulder has just been on leave' or 'Bill will be coming on leave'. So it seemed our paths were never to cross.

On my first night in KL I suggested to one of my armourer friends, a chap called Bert Findlay, that we should go and test the quality of the beer in the NAAFI. Bert was known to everyone as 'Kitchi' which means small in Malay. So Kitchi and I entered the NAAFI for the first time, purchased a couple of beers and found a vacant table. On the other side of the room was an airman whose face looked familiar. I couldn't settle so I went over to him and enquired *'I'm sure I know you. Is your name Faulder by any chance?* He replied *'Of course it bloody well is you daft bugger'.* At last we had met. Some 7000 miles from where we last spoke. It transpired that Bill was located in the ERS Unit which made complete sense given his engineering skills.

Life at the Unit was quite leisurely. The only significant change was that hitherto all physical work finished at 12noon. Now we worked until 4pm. Spare time in the evening could be spent in downtown KL. At some of the better class hotels dance bands played and petite

Chinese girls known as 'dancing partners' were provided for paying guests. At reception you could purchase a book of tickets and every time you danced with one of the girls you handed over a ticket. The dancer was paid a percentage of the value of the tickets she handed in. Contrary to what readers may be thinking, these dancing partners were not 'ladies of ill repute'. Many of them were earning money to have their children educated back in China.

On 10 October Kitchi, Taffy Williams, Bill Deacon, a Scotsman whose name eludes me and I were sent on detachment to No 151 Maintenance Unit at Seletar. We stayed in the transit camp where we had been on 25 August. Our job was to check all the spare stores and crate up for delivery to KL. One evening I decided to visit the main air base at Seletar and as usual went to the NAAFI. In the reading room in front of me was someone holding up a newspaper. Not just any newspaper. It was The Cumberland and Westmorland Herald, my local rag. The reader was hidden behind the paper but I decided I must speak to him. To my pleasant surprise it turned out to be a chap called Lonnie Robinson a hairdresser who was well known in Penrith. We talked for ages and he eventually loaded me up with several earlier copies of The Herald. These were most welcome as up to this point I hadn't received any mail from home. I was surprised to read that my sister Queenie had married on 4 October and even more surprised that my Dad had been found guilty in the local Police Court for accepting petrol coupons that had expired. The article suggested that he was convicted on a 'technicality'. Nevertheless he was guilty and the lads took great delight in telling everyone that my father was a jailbird.

Whilst at the main air base at Seletar we noticed that the so called 'front line' aircraft consisted only of a mere handful of Fairey Swordfish and Vickers Vildebeest biplanes and a couple of American Catalina flying boats. Not very re-assuring but I believe these were eventually supplemented by a number of American Brewster Buffalo fighters. More surprising was the work being undertaken by the Carpenters (Chippies) in their workshop. These Chippies were civilian, mainly Chinese, and were busy making full size replicas of the Brewster Buffaloes the purpose of which would soon become evident.

CHAPTER THREE

War begins – my first taste of 'Action'

Sunday 7 December 1941 will be remembered by many as the date of the Japanese bombing of Pearl Harbour. But they also attacked Singapore, Malaya and Hong Kong although the time difference meant that these attacks were recorded as 8 December 1941. This resulted in an immediate 'Declaration of War' on Japan by the Allies. This obviously affected the mood in camp but most remained calm and harboured the idea that 'all would be well in the end'. All was not well.

On 2 December (just five days before the attack on Pearl Harbour) the battleship HMS Prince of Wales and the battlecruiser HMS Repulse arrived in Singapore to re-inforce the Far Eastern Fleet. The arrival of these ships received a lot of publicity, the local radio proudly announcing that British power in this quarter of the globe was now invincible. Perhaps it would have been more prudent to keep quiet as on 10 December both ships were destroyed by Japanese aircraft off Kuantan in the South China Sea. This turned out to be the start of the worst single reverse that the British Empire ever suffered in war. Those highest in authority refused to accept that anything like that could happen. The then

Governor of Malaya, Sir Shenton Thomas, when told that the Japanese had landed at Kota Bharu some 400 miles to the north is understood to have said *'I trust you'll chase the little men off'*. They had in fact established a strong foothold within hours of landing and despite brave resistance by British troops they quickly broke through to the rear. This was the start of a pattern of panic by the British. Despite their numerical superiority they were reduced to a near rabble. The Japanese air offensive with regular attacks induced further fear and a blind urge to 'Get the hell out'.

On 27 December Kitchi, Bill Deacon, Taffy Williams and myself were ordered to assemble at short notice with side pack (knife, fork ,spoon, razor, toothbrush and comb) only. We travelled west by motor transport through a small town called Klang (which was to become familiar in January 1942) and on to the docks at Port Swettenham. We had in fact overshot our destination. As we alighted on to the dockside to have a quick 'recce' all hell broke loose. Nearby a battery of three Bofors light anti- aircraft guns were pumping shells into the air. We were in the middle of a Japanese air raid. Needless to say we didn't hang about and quickly retraced our steps. We arrived at a short landing strip on the right hand side of the road. There was one deserted building. We went to investigate and couldn't believe our eyes. There at the end of the landing strip were three full size replicas of the Brewster Buffalo fighter planes which the Chinese chippies had been making in the workshop at Seletar. It all became clear. They were simply decoys to fool the Japanese Spotter Planes on aerial reconnaissance. Worse was to follow – it was our job to go out daily and move the planes around to give the impression that they were being used. Not a job we really relished as it was reasonable to expect that we could be subject to attack by Jap planes.

We were billeted in the Anglo Indian School in Klang. One day we went from the Landing Strip back to the dockside at Port Swettenham. We were alerted by the sound of breaking glass which appeared to be coming from one of the Warehouses (Godown). We entered to discover that it was a Customs Bonded Warehouse where imported spirits and liquors were stored before being redeemed by the importer on payment of customs duty. Inside four British soldiers supervised by a Senior Army Officer were throwing each bottle most forcibly against the end wall of the building. By now there was a steady flow of liquid entering a drain on the outside of the building. It was a bit like entering a Scottish distillery, the aroma was enough to make you feel 'tiddly'. We heard on the grapevine that a Japanese landing was imminent so this 'criminal' action was necessary to prevent not only our troops but also the Japanese from acquiring the 'booty'. It was enough to make a confirmed spirit drinker weep.

Back in Klang there wasn't a single living sole to be found. All the civilians had been evacuated. It was most eerie. Only the odd dog, cat or hen was to be seen. Next to the School was a small Colonial type bungalow crammed full of high octane motor spirit. Taffy observed *'If that bloody lot goes up we will bloody well fry'*. The next day the skies were full of Japanese planes. Very un-nerving and by general consent, rightly or wrongly, we felt that it would be madness to go to the landing strip.

That evening a unit of Royal Artillery equipped with small field guns arrived. They said that they were running short of fuel at which point Taffy stood to his full height and shouted *'Don't you worry boyo we have just the thing'* and promptly broke into the bungalow and commenced wholesale distribution of the contents. The darkness was broken frequently by the most frightening noise of field gun shells being discharged. I readily admit to a feeling of instability tinged with out and out fright. Inwardly you feel frightened but you must not show it. This experience taught me a valuable lesson which I was able to rationalise as follows – *'Being brave is being frightened to say that you are frightened'*. So that when the going got tough you behaved out of character hopefully providing a positive effect on those around you.

On 3 January 1942 we were relieved to be recalled to KL. Not before time. We realised that New Year's Eve had passed without thought. Not surprising given all the deadly distractions. We subsequently learnt that our Royal Artillery had repelled an attempted Japanese landing on the west coast just north of Port Swettenham. Back in KL things had changed dramatically even though we had only been away for seven days. Our camp at Batu was now occupied by hundreds more airmen who had been re-located from 'up country'. Doubts were now starting to arise amongst those present as to the capability of the British to defend Malaya against such a cunning adversary. Mainly for the benefit of the Asiatic population the British Government persisted in propaganda that suggested all was still well even though the number of refugees was increasing daily and there was a swelling tide of wounded and demoralised servicemen displaying the pallor of exhausted and beaten men. The shape and contour of Malaya can be likened to the shape of an Indian club. Narrow at the top, narrowing just below centre and narrowing further at the base. On each coast the Japanese adopted a simple, but very effective, tactic. As soon as the British established a front line across the peninsula the Japanese landing parties moved further down the coast and landed geographically behind the British lines. In order not to be cut off by such a 'pincer' movement retreat was the only option. The increasing number of refugees included Government Officials and Tin Mining and Oil Drilling Engineers whose work places had been overrun by the advancing Japanese. For some strange reason nearly all of them were almost immediately enlisted into the services (mainly the RAF) and given officer rank. This caused a great deal of resentment amongst the trained service personnel as these individuals had no experience of service matters. They may have been 'managers' of men but they had no 'leadership' qualities so they commanded no respect and generally got in the way. Not exactly a morale booster and a rumour circulating (which turned out to be true) that some twenty four hours before the first bombs fell on Singapore a fleet of Japanese ships was currently off Cambodia Point on the southern tip of Indo China and heading towards Malaya was further demoralising. This fleet consisted of twenty eight troop carrying ships and it actually reached Kota Bharu on the north eastern coast of Malaya on 8 December (the same date as the bombing of Singapore). They came to anchor and at 1.15am soldiers of the Japanese Imperial Army began to pour ashore in rubber assault craft and so began the invasion of Malaya. The British propaganda machine still suggested all was well.

On 5 January and only two days after arriving back at KL we were under further movement orders. This time it was travel by a local commandeered bus with an RAF Transport driver. Train travel was impossible as all southbound trains were packed with refugees and Service personnel retreating from the Japanese advance. We were told that certain Regiments including British Indians were making heroic but largely unsuccessful stands against the advance. The roads were also choked with every type of vehicle escaping the advancing invader. Darkness and the drone of the bus engine were sleep inducing and even though the journey was quite winding and hilly most of us remained asleep until the bus came to a sudden halt. The driver had momentarily 'nodded off' and the bus was now hanging precariously on the edge of a deep ravine. Alighting from the normal front door was impossible as this would have meant stepping out into thin air. So we all alighted from the rear door where our 'difficult' situation soon became apparent. The bus needed to be winched from the rear. Several fully laden Chinese owned trucks passed by but in true Cumberland parlance they were not capable of 'pulling a clock hen off its nest'. Fortunately a large Thorneycroft from the service depot at Ipoh arrived on the scene and had little difficulty recovering our stranded bus. We resumed our journey with a different driver (I never did discover what happened to the original one) and as daylight broke we arrived at Seletar Transit Camp in Singapore where we had been on 25 August and 10 October. We remained here until 10

January during which time there were many Japanese bombing raids causing several civilian deaths.

On the morning of 10 January we travelled by bus through Singapore to Keppel Harbour. Earlier troopships from the UK and Middle East had arrived here too late resulting in many of those arriving almost literally walking into captivity. It also saw the sad parting of husband and wives, sweethearts and brothers and sisters as they sought escape by sea. Ships of all sizes were used for escape irrespective of their destination. The P & O Steamship Company was put in charge and insisted on a 'booking' system when it would have been far more sensible to simply load the ships with all the people they would hold to hasten departure. The dockside was also the scene of many bizarre occurrences which perhaps highlight the urgency of the situation. Civilians were driving up in brand new shiny motors and simply handing the ignition keys to any person who happened to be near before boarding their ship. Obviously applying the principle that 'Life comes first'. Some of the banks were hauling large crates of bank notes on to the quayside, placing them in the gutter and setting fire to them.

We de-bussed and marched along the quayside passing the towering troopships and the crowds of would be passengers arriving at a small coasting ship called – wait for it – MV Klang. This was to be our home for the next five days. MV Klang had a tonnage of 1100 tons which does not compare with the troopships loading behind us. She had a Chinese captain and three Chinese crew. She was coal fired so everywhere was grimy. Some of my colleagues noticed that the small rear hold of the ship had been loaded with service issue corned beef but, whether by design or accident, the coal for the ship had been tipped over it. We cast off and sailed past the island Belakang Mati (translated Behind the Dead). Sleeping was almost impossible as space was severely limited due to the sheer weight of numbers on board. At dawn we all became aware of the sound of an approaching aircraft. Without exception all of us on board were convinced that we were about to be attacked by the Japanese who were renowned for their low level machine gun attacks. The plane made a high pass then turned and came in lower to reveal (to the immense relief of everyone) Dutch insignia and therefore friendly. Apart from the vagaries of the tropical weather – Sun – Rain – Wind coupled with the salt spray the rest of the voyage passed without incident. The main complaint was the lack of proper toilet facilities and the absence of any washing facilities given the number of people on board. We followed a route between Banka Island and Sumatra mainland and then turned south crossing the Sunda Straits between Sumatra and Java where we had a close view of the volcanoes Krakatua and Anak Krakatua (Anak meaning child). Back in 1883 as many of you will recall Krakatua erupted with huge force claiming some 35,000 lives and at the same time created Anak Krakatua. We continued in an easterly direction along the southern seaboard of Java arriving at Cilacap (pronounced Chil-at-cap) on 15 January 1942. We sailed slowly into the harbour and tied up out in the river. We were told that on our right side was a convict settlement and were advised not to swim as the waters were crocodile infested. We would spend the night on board.

As I write this later (1988) and with information that

has since come to hand I am able to reflect on how lucky I was and what might have been. Many, many small ships such as ours had set out on a similar journey and with the same purpose. The losses were terrific. They were regularly bombed, shelled and machine gunned by the Japanese resulting in the occupants being cast into the sea with the minimum of life saving provision. Those who took to rafts or flotsam simply floated away to their deaths. Those that were lucky to reach many of the small islands had no food or water and were simply rounded up by the Japs and subjected to untold barbarity. Women and children were dealt with in the same manner as the Japs regarded them as the dregs of humanity. So why was I so lucky? Was it 'Divine Intervention?' There are three other occasions (which I mention later) which give rise to these thoughts. I am not particularly religious but being a Christian my religion is based on the adage *'Do as you wish to be done to'*. The presence of a God can sometimes be regarded as a fairy story but when something good happens (such as my safe arrival at Cilacap) it does raise the question 'Was it God's will?' When I reflect on my experiences I am happy to subscribe to it being 'God's will' that I survived but by the same token not even a devout Christian, be it layman, Archbishop or other member of the Clergy could explain why so many bright, strong, active and loyal young men paid the ultimate sacrifice.

The next day, 16 January, we disembarked and boarded a waiting train. It was fairly basic, shutters for windows and wooden planks for seats. One of our contingent had 'adopted' a small monkey which travelled with us. All exits had been closed to prevent its escape.

It spent most of its time swinging between the overhead luggage racks completing full circuits of the carriage. Whether due to fear or excitement it frequently urinated whilst completing its circuits much to the disgust of those on the receiving end. This continued for quite a while until an airman called Handforth, who I think hailed from Lancashire, shouted (and I quote) *'If you don't chuck that bugger out I will'*. Its adoptive parent was not really agreeable to this suggestion as it turned out he had 'rescued' it whilst in Cilacap. When we tied up in the harbour our ship was astern of an American Freighter. One of the American crewmen offered the monkey to anyone who was brave enough or daft enough to climb down our mooring ropes onto the mooring buoy and then up the mooring ropes of the American ship to collect the monkey which was imprisoned in a small sack. The would be 'monkey rescuer' took to the ropes and made rapid progress down to the mooring buoy. His modus operandi was to take hold of two adjacent ropes and keep himself on top of them. He assumed the same position on the ascent to the American Freighter and returned to the mooring buoy complete with 'bagged' monkey without difficulty. However, the ascent to our ship proved more difficult. The presence of the monkey was a hindrance and he was rapidly running out of steam. When he was about 3 yards from the ship, fatigue and gravity took over resulting in him swinging through 180° and having to hold on grimly with his hands and legs to prevent him falling into the waters below. Two of our crew saw his predicament and went down the ropes to his assistance and eventually hauled him and the monkey up the ropes to our ship. The 'monkey' rescuer was completely exhausted and frightened so after all his efforts he was not going to give the monkey up easily. Many of our contingent witnessed this adventure being acutely aware of the presence of crocodiles in the waters below had he fallen off the ropes. To satisfy any concerns that readers might have over the welfare of the monkey I have consulted my diaries and can confirm that the airman/monkey relationship still existed in December 1942 and probably beyond.

The train eventually arrived at Djocjakarta now spelt Yogyakarta (most place names were eventually renamed in 1972 to remove any connection with the previous Dutch influence). We alighted from the train, formed up and marched down Malioboro which is the main street of the town. It is suggested that the street was so named following an assault on Yogya by The Duke of Marlborough in 1812. We only marched a short distance before arriving at a school which fronted on to Malioboro. The gates swung open on to a sort of courtyard (probably the school playground). The yard was bounded on three sides by classrooms which were shaded by verandahs. Behind and to the left was another building which was to serve as our cookhouse and dining room. At the distant end were the school toilets. They deserve a mention. Whilst they were plumbed in to allow flushing they were devoid of pot and seat. Instead they had an eliptical hole in the base tiles with a raised tread strategically placed on either side of the hole. The user placed their feet on the raised treads, assumed a squatting position and hoped that their aim was good. Enough of that. The classrooms were provided with beds, lockers and mosquito nets. The railings and gate at the front of the school allowed an uninterrupted view of daily life on Malioboro. Immediately opposite was the Malang restaurant which proved to be an ideal place to spend ones off-duty time.

The next morning we marched back to the railway station where we boarded a three carriage train headed by a small wood fired locomotive which was revved up and raring to go. This was to be our daily routine for quite some time. What was remarkable about this journey was that the local signalman would authorise our departure on to the main eastbound line in the full knowledge that only one minute behind was the Surabaya express. This meant that our driver had to be 'on the ball' all the time in order to complete the five mile journey to the airfield at a place called Magoewa without impeding the following express. The airfield was served by a siding off the main line and quite often we would arrive in the siding only seconds before the express hurtled by. This almost daily occurrence meant that we were all conscious of the need for promptness and would chastise any member of our party who caused the slightest delay. We couldn't understand why the express was not allowed to go first.

At the airfield facilities were quite sparse. There was one medium sized hangar, an aircraft repair hangar, behind which was a compound secured by barbed wire for the storage of explosives and bombs. There was no runway only a grass covered airfield. No aircraft to be seen anywhere. Set back some distance from the airfield was an Engineering Machine Shop and on the perimeter was a 'shelter' constructed from bamboo and palm leaves. This was our dining hall where we were provided with packed lunches and mugs of tea made with evaporated milk. Why we were here was not immediately apparent. Our concerns were answered when several large four engine planes appeared over the horizon. They all circled the airfield and landed perfectly on the uneven grass surface. They were American Liberator and Super Fortress bombers of the 15th Bomber Group of the United States Air Force. We were, in our respective trades, to be attached to the Unit as ground crew. Quite re-assuring following the shortcomings observed previously in Malaya. You will recall that I was trained as an Armourer (Guns) by the RAF. After introduction to the US Aircrews and Supervisory Ground Crews it was clear that I was going to be used as an Armourer (Bombs) which was quite unsettling. Anyway, I was soon put to work 'Bombing Up' the aircraft. A Master Sergeant provided a demonstration on how this was to be done and made it clear that if mistakes were made when fusing the bombs there would be no second chance. The job required a high level of skill and concentration. The bombs were brought by trailer from the compound. They were marked 300 kgs (about 650 lbs). Briefly, the role entailed fitting the tail fin (a simple task), checking the detonator apertures at both the nose and tail ends of the bomb with a special gauge to ensure that the detonators could be safely inserted without the risk of premature detonation. Each detonator had a small aperture through which was passed a strong steel wire with a central loop. Each bomb was then winched into the bomb racks on the aircraft and attached to the trigger hooks whilst the wire loops were attached to separate hooks slightly above. This arrangement meant that if the pilot wished to jettison his bombs then both sets of hooks were opened allowing the bombs to fall disarmed with the wire still intact. If they were to be dropped in anger then only the bomb hooks were opened and the bombs would fall 'armed' causing a double explosion on impact. The American Aircrew were completely open about their mission. It was to be dawn and dusk bombing of Japanese positions at Balikpapan on Borneo. The US Air Force had suffered heavy losses of aircraft on the ground at Pearl Harbour so we were told that in the event of an alert involving a likely Japanese air raid then all planes, irrespective of their state of readiness, must take off immediately and fly out over the ocean until the alert was over. With this in mind there were several occasions when we simply had to abandon what we were doing as the priority was to get the planes in the air as quickly as possible. We would then watch as the planes took off and quite often it was clear that some of the bomb-laden planes did not have either the speed or the elevation to clear some large palm trees at the end of the airstrip so the pilot quickly jettisoned the bombs on to the airfield. The day's work undone in a second!

Despite the threat of frequent Japanese air raids we still enjoyed our free time in the evening. The local restaurants were a favoured haunt. They served various dishes many with a Dutch influence. 'Flensjes met Gelei' thin pancakes with jam. 'Pannekoeken' thick pancakes with savoury filling. The beer was 'Anker Donker' a dark beer which was quite palatable. At the other end of Malioboro was Bruins restaurant which was very popular so we quickly changed this to 'The RAF Restaurant'. Not for long, as it soon became popular with the Americans following their arrival so its name was changed to 'The United States Restaurant'. We concluded that the Americans must be the big spenders.

We still experienced Japanese air raids but they tended to be by solitary planes so not much damage was inflicted. However, the Americans felt that bigger things were to come so they planned to re-locate all their bombers to North Australia. It was also proposed that as we had worked so well with the American aircrew we would re-locate with them. Tremendous news. Spirits rose immediately. However, the joint Far East Command made up of various 'rag tag' separate forces known as A,B,C,D (American, British, Chinese, Dutch) scuppered the whole idea. The bombers left.

This almost coincided with the fall of Singapore to the Japanese and more significantly a small but successful Jap landing on the North Coast of West Java. So the Americans were wise to re-locate. The quote *'He who fights and runs away, lives to fight another day'* is very apposite here.

The following few days were very uncertain and at this time we had a visit from a lady who, many years ago, had arrived in the East Indies from Cornwall. She was a very active member of an organisation called 'Leger des Heils' which translates literally as Army of Saviours and is the Dutch arm of The Salvation Army. She was a most devout lady with a big heart. She invited us to visit her home the next evening where she would serve Cornish Pasties, her pride and joy. Three of us attended and were made most welcome. We were served cups of tea followed by the Cornish Pasties as promised. God bless her, but they were awful. She had either lost her touch or was unable to source the right ingredients. All three of us agreed and not wishing to offend her consigned the said pasties to our handkerchiefs and then pockets whilst she was out of the room brewing the second cups of tea. We had to politely refuse when she offered us a second one. It was quite obvious that she enjoyed our company and many times I have wondered what ever became of her as events unfolded.

The Japanese landings on Java referred to earlier had begun on 1 March 1942. Reports at the time suggested that they had met with stiff resistance but they still seemed to make remarkable progress. On 2 March we received short notice Orders that we were to be drafted into the British and Dutch Infantry. We were issued with short Lee Enfield rifles and ammunition an action that perhaps highlighted our present position. We travelled by rail to a town called Poerballinga. The town's geographical location indicated that we were headed in the general direction where it was 'all happening'. We were accommodated in large bamboo rice drying sheds. Here we were given more arms drill by an NCO of the Argyll and Sutherland Highlanders. Next day we moved only a short distance (leaving our kit behind) to a long steel railway bridge spanning a wide river. We sat in what appeared to be previously dug slit trenches. Nothing happened during daylight. In the tropics there is no twilight. Darkness is almost immediate. Once darkness fell, sniper fire from the opposite bank of the river began. We were ordered not to return fire even though there was a strong desire to do so. Our infantry NCO then explained that on the next volley from the opposite bank we should return fire at once aiming at their gun flashes and having fired move quickly as the enemy would do exactly the same, aiming at our gun flashes. This went on for a very long time and I confess that I was frightened. It was my first experience of combat. Just before daylight, the firing ceased completely and was followed by an eerie silence broken only by monkeys chattering loudly high in the trees above. We were ordered to return to the rice sheds and on leaving saw for the first time that the bridge was packed with gelignite charges with all the fuse wires running back to our embankment. It soon became clear that the Dutch Forces were operating their 'Scorched Earth' policy frequently employed in the European Theatre of war. In the event of further advances by the Japanese this bridge any many others would be destroyed to impede their progress. We repeated defence of the bridge for the next two (long) nights. The Japs continued to fire at us but made no attempt to cross the river. This worried me and even though I was a young and inexperienced combatant I felt in my own mind that they were simply a decoy and that the main body of Japs would cross the river either higher up or lower down and close in behind us to cut off any retreat. Fortunately it never happened. Through the daytime sleep was very difficult due to the dirty state of the rice shed earth floor and the possibility of being overrun by the Japs. The pre-darkness 'fall-in' was the same as previous days but this time an Officer said that a crossing of the river by the Japs was highly likely BUT he had received a message to the effect that if we could make our way safely to the camp at Cilacap (where we had arrived on 15 January) there would be sea transport available to enable us to evacuate Java. This acted as a morale booster. We almost cheered. It was also explained that the natives were not to be trusted as they would turn anyone in for a bowl of rice. So secrecy, stealth and silence were the order of the day. It puzzled me how secret information could be sent and received and also how rail transport could be arranged.

On that note the Senior British Officer asked a most ridiculous question *'Is there anyone here who can drive a locomotive?'* You felt like saying *'Don't be daft'* but as you have guessed by now up spoke a little Geordie Airman *'Why aye man ah can do just that but a'll need a stoker'*. There was no shortage of volunteers for that position. So the Loco driver and his stoker, accompanied by two armed men, set off along the rail track on foot. We then had another briefing. Everyone gave it their undivided attention. Once on the move there had to be complete silence, no smoking and no lights whatsoever. The Japanese tactic was to occupy positions at the top of railway cuttings and on the arrival of a train to ambush it with intense machine gun and mortar fire showing no mercy and taking no prisoners. Not very re-assuring!

After what seemed an age and after the fall of darkness we saw a red glow in the distance. It was the train travelling backwards with sparks flying from the funnel. A bit if a contradiction given that we had to show no lights yet the sparks were highlighting the very presence of the train. The Geordie driver (I wish I could remember his name) jumped from the footplate and momentarily joined his section mates and asked them to take care of his kit as he couldn't take it in the locomotive. He also said, and these are his exact words as I will remember them to my dying day *'The reason they wanted a driver and stoker was cos the Wogs had simply buggered off'*. The loco was wood fired and when the fire was being 'drawn' to create steam for the boiler the extra draught caused sparks to shoot out of the smoke stack. Everyone boarded the train in an orderly fashion. It is remarkable how disciplined people are when survival is paramount. We set off with a minimum of noise and progressed slowly. We had been travelling quite some time when there was an almighty flash and explosion. We all grabbed our firearms expecting an attack only to realise that it was a terrific thunder clap immediately above us and as is normal in the tropics the thunder and lightning occur almost simultaneously. What a relief. We continued slowly in the knowledge that the bridges were mined and that the track could be compromised in places. At daybreak we finally came to a halt on the dockside at Cilacap almost precisely where we had boarded the train for Yogyakarta on 16 January. We were met by a small Flight Lieutenant RAF. He was livid and greeted us with '*You're far too bloody late. The fucking ship couldn't wait. It set sail some time ago*'. Despair and despondency spread like the plague. Conversation was minimal and what was said was hardly complimentary. It was difficult to apportion blame. Perhaps the message to evacuate Poerballinga had simply taken too long to percolate through. Whilst at Poerballinga I sorted out my kit. I had a side pack, a back pack and two kit bags. In kit bag No 2 I packed the kit that was least important to me. In kit bag No 1 I packed belongings slightly more important to me and so on leaving my side pack with my most valued possessions. So today was the day I would ditch kit bag No 2. We were sat on the dockside waiting further developments. There was an air of disorganisation and uncertainty. Then there was an unholy explosion out at sea. It turned out to be a ship called The City of Manchester which had exploded after being torpedoed by the Japanese. It was the very ship that we had failed to catch. It appears that the Japs had been 'sitting' out at sea waiting for the ship to sail into its torpedo sights. Simple. It is reasonable to speculate that the native Fifth Column had simply advised the Japs of the ships departure so its fate was already decided before it sailed. Earlier I referred to 'Divine Intervention' and that there were four occasions when I regarded my survival as more than good fortune. Well this was number two. As a non- swimmer on board that ship what chance of survival would I have had if I had been dumped into the Indian Ocean. I leave the reader to speculate.

We received instructions that we could march to a Dutch Army Barracks not too far away where we would be fed. This is the point at which I jettisoned kit bag No 2 (all part of my plan). We marched along the docks and were aware of a solitary plane high in the sky. It was a Japanese spotter plane. As we approached the entrance to the Barracks we became aware of a heavy droning sound increasing in volume second by second. As we looked skywards we saw an unbelievable sight. Moving across the sky were lots of Japanese heavy bombers. They were travelling in an arrowhead formation at not too fast a speed. Each arrowhead was made up of twenty seven planes (yes we had time to count them) and there were eight such formations all heading in our direction. We quickly calculated that there were over two hundred planes and they weren't on their way to a garden party! So we all rushed for cover. I shot into an air raid trench just inside the barracks. For some reason the trench was lined with horse hair. I never did discover why. The leading plane in each formation suddenly let off a burst of machine gun fire. This was clearly a signal for all the other planes to release their deadly bombs. As it was daylight and despite its seriousness it was captivating to see the falling bombs glinting in the sunshine. Some were falling in the normal way whilst others were tipping end over end. As they hit the ground it shook unbelievably followed by palls of thick smoke. In the sky were puffs of black smoke from the British Ack-Ack guns. Unfortunately these were bursting at a comfortable distance behind the planes as the British guns had no sighting equipment. I learnt later that they were located on a school playing field and had received a direct hit. The bombers continued on their murderous journey and were quickly followed by a wave of Jap dive bombers. These were something new to us. We witnessed their abnormally steep descent and as they disappeared below the near horizon of coconut palms we cheered presuming that our Ack-Ack guns had got them. How wrong we were. The explosion with the attendant ground tremor was not that of a crashing plane but a dive bomber releasing its deadly load.

Despite all the intervening years and the fact that 'all hell was breaking loose' around me I can still recall other less important and sometimes humorous events which occurred. For example, at the entrance to the barracks there was a deep drain running parallel to the road. In it was laid a pipe of about 18 inches diameter. When the Jap bombers attacked an elderly and rather portly RAF Flight Leiutenant called Harris (he was an ex planter co-opted into the RAF) chose the pipe as a place to shelter. Unfortunately the pipe's diameter could not accommodate his portly frame so he was left with his expansive posterior exposed. Not a pretty sight.

The regular Officers were keen to try and impose some order so they called 'Fall-In' and we formed up on the roadway. Whilst assembling we saw clearly the aftermath of the bombing. There were fires everywhere and many buildings had been flattened. At the same time an open backed British Army wagon approached with its horn sounding constantly. As it passed the site and smell was quite sickening. Its passengers were members of the Ack-Ack crew that had received a direct hit which I mentioned earlier. The driver being unfamiliar with the area was urgently seeking a hospital or field ambulance station. As it turned out I was to meet two of the injured passengers in July 1942.

We then marched back to the railway station at the dockside which we had left earlier. It was a lovely day but the area around the station had been devastated by the bombing. At the station was a pile of baggage in exactly the same place as it had been unloaded from the train earlier. And sure enough there was my kit bag No 2 which I had abandoned earlier. This prompted me to think 'What had happened to our train? Had the bold Geordie driven it away to safety? We will never know. We were told that we were to be a 'baggage party' responsible for recovering the items left behind when we marched off for breakfast that morning. The Officer in Charge of our party produced several full crates of Tiger Beer (a brew from Singapore which is widely available nowadays) and encouraged us to drink. His motive soon became clear. We weren't a 'baggage party' at all. We had to recover the bodies of those killed in the raid. By now I had reached the ripe old age of eighteen years and eleven months and had never encountered a corpse before. It appears that it was customary to provide alcohol to those 'lads' involved in body recovery to promote 'Dutch Courage' and it turned out that any stronger stuff had suffered the same fate as that in the bonded warehouse at Port Swettenham which I described earlier. So we had to make do with Tiger beer.

On the station platform was one male body. It was badly charred. The station itself had only been hit by shrapnel. There were no signs of fire. It soon became apparent what had happened. The man was the Stationmaster, a Javanese. During the raid he had taken shelter and when all was clear he had come outside and stepped on a live electric cable which had been brought down during the raid. Our next encounter was in the area outside the station. Here there was a slit trench shelter. A bomb had exploded alongside the trench and had almost filled it with earth. Here there were three bodies, one white and two coloured. The white man's left leg had been severed just below his hip. His shirt had been blown away by the blast and there was a large shrapnel wound in the back of his head. I was paired up with a tall blonde haired man from East Anglia. I mention him for reasons I will explain later. Now seeing the mutilated body of a fellow human being is one thing but having to pick it up tests your resolve to the limit all the time having to resist the urge to vomit, Tiger beer or no Tiger beer. In short, we completed the job and found a stand pipe where we had a good wash down.

We then returned to where our kit had been left (it was under guard and quite safe) where we were told that we would be moving on to obviate the danger caused by sudden air raids. Anything transportable had to be taken and we were instructed to walk in single columns on either side of the road not more than ten paces apart. This reduced the risk of heavy losses if we were marching in 'Column of Route'. It was still a lovely day but the heat was intense. We drank milk from newly fallen coconuts to quench our thirst but this was later discouraged as it causes diarrhoea and prickly heat. By using the sun as a tracking device it was clear that we were headed roughly in a north westerly direction and away from the coast. This was quite unsettling as we were heading back towards Poerballinga where we had encountered the Japs at the river bridge. If they had advanced, as most likely, we would encounter them even sooner!

Official information was non- existent and we were completely unaware who was making the decisions. We never did find out. Just before the fall of darkness it started raining, not very heavy just a steady drizzle but it was still uncomfortable. When we reached a small level crossing over a single railway line we bedded down for the night on what appeared to be the verandah of the crossing keeper's shack. My kit bag No 1 had become heavier due to the rain so I decided to abandon this one too. Several thoughts also occurred. Was this the railway line that we had travelled down the previous day? Where were the Japs right now? The jungle encroached almost to the edge of the railway line on both sides so the Japs could sneak up on us almost undetected. Not very re-assuring. The last two days had taken a heavy toll on most of us. Even the strongest and hardiest admitted to fatigue and a feeling of hopelessness. The rain persisted throughout the night but stopped just before daybreak. When the sun came out the humidity increased to an unbearable degree and the lack of any washing facilities added to our discomfort.

It was now 7 March 1942. We were ordered to march on but this time to follow the railway line. Again using the sun as a compass and noting that we were following a series of left hand curves I was able to deduce that we were headed in roughly a westerly direction. We plodded on and all the time I felt that we were exposed and vulnerable to ambush by the Japs. At one point I was joined by the tall blonde chap from East Anglia who I mentioned earlier. He said *'I've been looking all over for you'*. I asked him why. He said *'Well, you remember in the air raid when we were in the slit trenches at the barracks and later when we worked together at the station yesterday, well, I was dead scared until I looked at you and saw how cool, calm and collected you were. Well that re-assured me and made me get a grip of myself'*. I was amazed because truthfully I was probably more scared than him but I didn't make him any wiser. As I said earlier *'Being brave is being afraid to admit that you are afraid'*. So let it be. Progress became slower and every hour the 'column' became longer because of the stragglers. There was a distinct possibility that the back markers would become detached from the main body and be left behind. However, the main complaint (apart from not knowing what was going on) was the lack of any organised kitchen or food supplies. Rounding yet another curve we came upon a set of points which converted the track into a double track. Was this just a passing place or better still a station? Thankfully it turned out to be the latter. If there was a station there was most likely a town or village. It was a place called Ciamis (pronounced Cham-iss) and in the station was a train complete with locomotive in full steam. As we walked along the platform we passed the locomotive and there stood on the footplate was the bold 'Geordie' complete with grimy face from his endeavours. A lot of the 'lads' broke ranks and asked him *'Have we to get on board?'* Others asked *'Where are we going?'* With a broad grin the 'Geordie' replied *'So far as I know we aren't going anywhere'* and then pointed in the direction of our 'Tea Planter' Officers saying *'None of these buggers know where the hell they're bloody going but I'm keeping a head of steam up just in case!'*

Instead of boarding the train we marched into the small town arriving at a sizeable building which served as a cinema. There were no seats and for that matter no lights so visibility could only be achieved by leaving all the doors open. Here we were served with Machonocies tinned onion soup. At home in my pre-war days I had a silly and unfounded dislike of onions or any food that had been anywhere near onions. I must owe my mother a thousand apologies for my behaviour whenever she served up anything remotely connected with onions. Here, food was simply food and there were no conditions attached to eating it. Without hesitation I consumed the soup, onions and all. It was most welcome and I have been a devotee of onions ever since. Despite the impression given by 'Geordie' that the train was going to depart at any minute we were reliably informed that we would be here for at least one night. We were told not to leave the building as we were about to be briefed by the Officer in Charge. This he did. He was called Ballinger and had been the Stores Officer at KL. He started rather hesitantly and said words along the lines of *'Now we've all heard of the British Lion and how it bares its teeth when cornered'* and went on *'As you know in these conditions reliable and up to date information is most scant. What we do know is that the*

Japanese advances from the north to the south have been disastrously swift. The area where we have just arrived from is threatened within hours. So in the morning we will attempt to make good our departure towards the west by train. The outcome we cannot guess but this I must say to you and it is not very heroic. If you fall into the hands of the Japanese you must destroy and dispose of all weapons and ammunition and any knives with blades over four inches long. Finally (and to our great surprise) if you choose to make your own escape into the jungle when circumstances dictate, then you may do so, but I am bound to remind you that you are Europeans in a foreign country where there are those who would turn you in for a tin of rice'. The effect was electric. There was almost complete silence borne of a sense of hopelessness. Sleep was fitful but welcome after the events of the last two days.

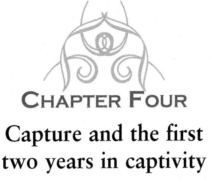

CHAPTER FOUR

Capture and the first
two years in captivity

Sunday 8 March 1942 came as all others had done with one notable exception. Not one man needed prompting to return to the train and get on board. As we boarded the tall blonde man from East Anglia approached and said '*I was looking for you last night. I've found your kit bag and brought it to the cinema*'. I daren't tell him that I was trying to get rid of the bloody thing. The train pulled slowly out of the station piloted by 'Geordie'. Progress was intentionally slow and conversation almost nil. Last night's information had sapped the resolve of even the strongest of wills. No one would admit it but we were like a boxer out on his feet waiting for his seconds to throw the towel in. We eventually arrived at some sidings and then entered a station. It was called Tasikmalaya. We stopped. We hadn't been stopped long when the stationmaster came and told us that the Japs were only two miles away in the direction from which we had come. We found this hard to believe given that our journey had been uneventful. At that same moment we saw a train arriving in reverse from the opposite direction. The passengers on this train advised us that they had returned because the Japs were only one and a half miles away in that direction. This was it. What happens next? Flight Lieutenant Ballinger ordered us to leave the station and go to a deep river where we were to dispose of all arms and equipment. This was awful as it was done in full view of the inquisitive locals. Having completed this we then sat on the roadside along from the station. After a few minutes three Japanese light tracked vehicles came into view. They were very similar to Bren carriers, they may even have been formerly British owned. Behind these followed a camouflaged open topped staff car flying the Jap flag. It contained two officers. We were ordered to stand up and the senior RAF Officer saluted the two officers who returned the salute and gave a slight bow. BUT THEY DIDN'T STOP! I don't know what we expected but everyone was saying 'Well *what do we do now?*' Over the years since the war many historians have said that no-one was more surprised at the whirlwind success of the invasion than the Japs themselves. So much so that the 'crack' front line Jap troops simply returned to their points of landing to await their next objective. Also it has been said that if it had been possible to re-mobilise the Allies, and I stress if it had been possible, then the outcome might have been quite different. Two of our Officers returned to the station and advised that they had found a billet at a nearby racecourse. We took up residence. Until now Bill Faulder had been compelled to stay with his own ERS Unit but here we met up and agreed to share our scant resources. Our pitch was to be on the concrete steps of the tiered grandstand. We had no bedding and concrete can be very hard. We did have one gas cape between us. Hobson's Choice. We will both have to sleep under it.

We decided to have a look round. There was a short lane as an entrance. There were two rows of stables (I think we may call them loose boxes) which were quite clean. There was a series of long troughs with a piped water supply. These would serve as our washing facilities. There were some water closets (Java Style) but these were completely insufficient for our numbers. Whilst looking round who should we bump into but Ferdie Litherland, he of finger bowl fame. He was with the GES Section and hadn't changed one bit. We ventured out on to the race track itself. It resembled a paddi field as it was covered in so much water. On the track was a very sobering sight. There we saw a British 3.7 inch anti- aircraft gun. Its long barrel was pointing skywards but its end was peeled back like a banana skin. Attached to the firing mechanism was a length of camouflage tape about twenty yards in length. At the far end of the tape was a shallow grave marked with a rough cross. The grave was itself waterlogged. It soon became clear what had happened. The gun had been loaded firstly with a shell point inward and then a second shell loaded in the breach block in the ordinary way. The length of the tape was to allow the 'firer' to be far enough away from the double explosion. Clearly not. His war was over. As my mother would have said '*He was somebody's son*'.

For the next few days we led a Jap-less life which was uncanny. Natives were allowed to sell their wares and they squatted along one side of the entrance lane. There was no shortage of things to buy and no shortage of money either. One day an airman called Hatcher (a Channel Islander) went to buy a large tin of butter (yes tinned butter). After some haggling with the vendor a deal was struck. Hatcher returned to his billet and promptly emptied the butter into his 'Dixie' and then filled the empty butter tin with soil. He then returned to the area where the vendors were located with the butter tin hidden behind his back. He selected a different vendor who was selling the same brand of butter and asked to see it. He declined the purchase and handed back the tin full of soil. Two for the price of one! But it doesn't end there. One of our lads then went to the vendor who had been cheated and purchased a tin of butter. And, yes, you've guessed it, he got the one full of soil! He went straight back to the vendor to complain. The vendor was completely puzzled but reluctantly handed over a proper one. How to impress the locals!

At 11am that day the Dutch High Command signed a Decree of Capitulation to the Japanese Imperial Army. This was completed at the aerodrome at Kalajati, Bandung. So this was final. We had surrendered. But where were the Japs?

At the racecourse we began to get organised. We set up a sick bay. We acquired some Dutch Army field kitchens and designated an area as the Cookhouse. We heard on the grapevine that the vanguard of our unit, travelling a few hours behind from Poerballinga (as we had done) was ambushed by the Japs at the side of the rail track. The train had been 'raked' with machine gun fire. It increased speed before the second attack but this time it was hit by mortar fire and came to a standstill. Some of the troops escaped and fled along the track to a bridge which had already been mined. The Dutch forces thought that this was the Japs advancing and blew up the first span whilst our lads were still on it. A Dutch

Officer realising the mistake actually pulled out the burning fuses with his bare hands.

Things continued as normal in the camp. One day the Officers laid on a sports day in an attempt to boost morale. Enthusiasm was difficult to raise but rather strangely on the same day a small contingent of Japanese soldiers marched down the road and right past our camp. It was difficult to work out what was going on. But on 24 March we had a visit from a Japanese NCO who advised that we would be moving tomorrow morning but didn't say where. That night I had a dream that we had returned to Yogyakarta and back to the school on Malioboro but the beds had been removed and replaced by straw. I told Bill about this but he just laughed.

It was four thirty in the morning of 25 March when we were awakened. It was cold and gloomy. The degree of silence was quite tangible, caused, I think, by the uncertainty of not knowing what was happening and where we were going to. We were on the move, that was clear, but this was preceded by a 'roll call' (tenko in Japanese) which was to become an annoying and regular part of our lives. As daylight broke we found ourselves back at Tasikmalaya railway station. *At this point I would just like to add that on 16 August 1988 I re-visited this very same railway station with my grandson. Forty six years, five months and nine days since I first arrived here on 8 March 1942. I was overcome with emotion as here I stood in that very same place as I had all those years ago – a distant day that had such a lasting and permanent effect on the rest of my life. Interestingly, the station had not changed at all.* Japanese guards were posted at regular intervals at the station entrance. This was the first time we had seen our captors at close sight. We boarded the train which was waiting in the station. It was facing in a different direction to that of 'Geordie's' train when we arrived on that momentous Sunday. The locomotive was now in the charge of two Javanese men. We moved off. There was a Jap guard at each end of the train which was not over-crowded. We passed the local aerodrome where we learnt there was another two thousand British prisoners. After what seemed only a short time the train stopped. We looked out to see a wide slow moving river. We also saw the remains of a three span steel bridge. The furthest span had been destroyed with the railway lines hanging festooned over the gap. Could it be the bridge that we had defended? We had only seen it in darkness so it was difficult to tell. Likewise it could also have been the site of the later ambush. To cross the river we had to use large canoes, each holding about twenty men. The technique was to commence upstream, reach the mid-point of the river and then let the current take over whilst steering to the opposite bank. When it was my turn to board a canoe I caught my watch with my back-pack losing the glass and the minute hand. What good was a watch without a minute hand? On every journey two of the less fortunate of our lot had to ferry the canoe back for the next load. Fortunately, I wasn't one of them. On the far side of the bridge another train was waiting for us to continue our journey. We boarded, but as the ferrying process took quite a long time to complete we remained stationary for an age. The temperature inside the train became unbearably hot and stifling. We were given 'lunch', four biscuits and a piece of cheese. Nothing to drink!

At ten minutes past three on the station clock we clambered out of the train at Yogyakarta railway station. We had been here before but this time the circumstances were entirely different. We went out on to the road where we were required to line up. We then marched off with Jap guards alongside us. We turned right at the level crossing and as we passed the RAF and USAF restaurants the locals were lined four deep on each side of the road. A strange emotion came over me. Not one of shame in defeat but difficult to explain. At the head of the column was a brash Irishman called Paddy Burke who was in Bill Faulder's Engine Repair Unit. Almost as one and led by Paddy we broke into song, *'There'll always be an England'*. No doubt inspired by this the locals began to cheer and some even waved Union Jacks. We couldn't understand it. We hadn't won the war (yet), we were prisoners. The Japs themselves didn't know how to react. They simply stared straight ahead and refused to acknowledge the cheers. We marched on down the main street of Malioboro and turned left into the very same school that we had occupied when stationed here previously. We were allocated classrooms (billets) at which point I turned to Bill and said *'Now what about my dream. The same place but the beds have gone'*. *'Ah'* replied Bill *'But there's no straw, it looks as if we will have to sleep on the deck'*. At that moment a bullock cart trundled through the front gate and completed my dream by unloading a load of STRAW.

At the time of our previous stay here I befriended a Eurasian family named Brett (mother and daughter). The daughter was called Ferry. They lived in a street called Gowongan Lor. On our first evening back at the school several locals appeared at the railings to see if they could renew old acquaintances despite there being two guards on duty. Ferry was no exception. I gave her my damaged wrist watch to see if she could get it repaired. The Japs did not attend on us but two days later I was to have my first 'encounter' with one of these Oriental Gentlemen. Ferry had come to the railings to tell me that the watch could not be repaired. At the same time a car pulled up and a Japanese Officer stepped out (I concluded this as he was wearing a sword but was to learn later that swords are worn by Sergeant Major upwards). Ferry quickly disappeared. The Jap started shouting but at the time I didn't realise that his words were directed at me. I was more interested in his dress – black leather calf length boots, dark brown riding breeches, khaki shirt with red badges of rank on the collar and finally the customary peaked cap. Within two strides he was into the school compound. He walked straight up to me and with direct eye contact delivered a diatribe of which I didn't understand one word. As a first eyeball to eyeball encounter I was left in no doubt as to his intentions as he then produced a pencil and promptly drew a half inch circle over my left breast. He then marched out of the gate from whence he had come. The circle must surely mean that I was to be shot for fraternising with the locals. Needless to say my shirt was washed with great haste. Several of our lads had witnessed this and immediately christened the Jap 'Gumbooto'. Obviously, nothing ever became of this otherwise I wouldn't be writing this but it did give rise to some amusing thoughts. After this initial encounter with the Jap Officer I noticed that every sword carrying Jap had great difficulty coping with this appendage due to their small stature and the length of the sword. To prevent the sword tip touching the ground they had to keep one hand on the hilt and push it forward meaning that they never had two hands free. Very amusing but to laugh at them would have been fatal.

Within the next seventy two hours we received an order that we were required to work at an airfield. It turned out to be the airfield at Magoewa where we had worked previously with the USAF. Ironically, we were to travel on that same little train as we had previously so in that respect nothing had changed. Our job was to fill in all the craters on the airfield to make it serviceable again. We had the use of an ex British Army Dodge truck which was used to deliver soil and stones which were tipped into the craters. Our job was to consolidate the mass by jumping up and down on it until it was as level as a billiard table. This took a number of days and each time we were supervised by a Jap guard. The accepted procedure was that the Jap guard had to indicate that he was happy with the work done on a particular crater before we were allowed to move on to the next one. It didn't take long to work out that the average Jap soldier was quite dumb and could be made to believe almost anything. One day we had an RAF Warrant Officer called Bardsley in charge of our crater filling party. He said *'Watch me. I'm going to have this little bugger on a string'*. He indicated to the Jap that he felt that work on a crater had been completed when clearly it needed at least another six inches of infill and made to move on to the next crater. At this point the Jap got all excited and even though he was speaking in Japanese it was clear that he felt that aeroplanes landing would tip on to their noses when landing. Bardsley knew exactly what he meant but reckoned not to understand.

The Jap passed his rifle to Bardsley and retreated about fifteen yards. Then with arms outstretched he ran towards the crater making an aeroplane noise. At the edge of the hole he stopped and did a hand stand with his nose to the ground. Bardsley motioned that he now fully understood and promptly continued to fill the crater.

This amusing little cameo and other similar occurrences gave rise to the feeling that most Jap soldiers lacked the ability to think for themselves and blindly accepted orders from senior command no matter how dangerous or difficult. The 'kamikaze' pilots, perhaps, demonstrate this perfectly although we weren't aware of them at this time. Part of the Japanese psyche – loyalty in the extreme to their Emperor, where death was seen as an honour. An approach which may account for their lightning success in East Asia.

Another difficulty affecting the Jap Guard/POW relationship was the language barrier. This gave rise to several confrontations resulting in frequent beatings. English speaking people are known for their 'reluctance' to learn a foreign language as it is so widely spoken expecting in turn that the foreigner had learnt English. This didn't work with the Jap guards as they spoke little or no English so they had great difficulty getting the POW's to understand their instructions. Even though there was a willingness to comply the lack of understanding caused the Japs to get more and more agitated and coupled with their notorious short temper frequently resulted in a beating.

One day whilst working on crater filling duties W O Bardsley sidled up to me and said '*Smudger, keep your bloody head down, your friend Gumbooto is coming over*. I didn't need to be told twice. In my mind (quite laughable now) I thought this is it. I'm for the firing squad. It couldn't be further away from the truth. He had come to tell Bardsley that we would shortly be on the move again. When we were made aware of this we all felt that our twice a day march between the school and the railway station was becoming too popular with the 'locals' who were always present to watch these daily events. Perhaps our singing of patriotic songs added to the attraction.

One evening we had returned to the school and went to the cookhouse to collect our usual boiled rice (which the Dutch aptly called 'Pap'). As normal we formed an orderly queue when all of a sudden one of the windows of the room was thrown open to reveal a very angry Jap Officer with sword drawn. No-one present was aware of the reason for his rage. He jumped from the window into the room, lifted his sword above his head and brought it down with a rapid sweep aimed at one of our lads. It was only by good fortune that it missed and ended up cutting a deep swathe into an empty table. After the initial shock had subsided we concluded that his anger was probably as a result of us not acknowledging his presence. Whenever a Jap Officer arrived we had been instructed to make a polite bow from the hips with hands by the sides and fingers outstretched. Arising from this incident WO Bardsley was informed by the Aerodrome Commander that we were shortly to receive a visit from a very high ranking Jap Officer who had advised that from now on we were to use Japanese words of command for saluting etc. Obviously as a direct result of the sword incident. '*Kiotsuke*' (pronounced key-yot-sookay) means attention. '*Kire*' (pronounced Ki-ray) means salute – a sharp forward movement from the hips. '*Yasume*' (pronounced Yass-may) means stand at ease but can also mean 'rest'. The Aerodrome Commander arrived and strutted from gang to gang impersonating the expected visitor. We responded to a lot of '*Kiotsuke*' and '*Kire*' until he was satisfied that we had met the required standard and employed the correct degree of bow.

The high ranking visitor turned out to be a Japanese Naval Commander and at the time of his arrival we were in the middle of a '*Yasume*' sitting on our shovels and eating sugar cane. We sprung to *Kiotsuke* and *Kire'd* but the seriousness of the occasion eluded us. The Naval Commander delivered a speech in average English. He advised that a decisive sea battle was in progress off the coast of Australia and because the outcome was to be a Japanese victory he expressed deep sorrow for our plight and sympathy for our families. He advised us to make the best of our lives as we would be prisoners for ten and a half years. We christened him the 'Mad Captain'.

On 21 April, my nineteenth birthday (my twentieth service birthday), we were on the move as had been advised. We boarded the little train for the last time and alighted, as usual, at the aerodrome. We marched to the old Dutch workshops at the end of the airfield. Seeing was believing. The Dutch had placed explosive charges everywhere. Some hadn't exploded. Most had and had caused extensive damage to the roof. The weather had broken suddenly and the downpour had resulted in pools of water lying inside the building. We all had a straw bed mat and a single sheet (donated by the locals) and there was soon a scramble for bed spaces. Also we soon realised that we would be sharing the building with a considerable number of rats. Was the 'Mad Captain' responsible for this? Did he want to sever our connection with the friendly 'locals' and more importantly sap our morale? Frankly the latter was almost true as there was in the region of three hundred of us sharing totally inadequate accommodation.

Next day our task was to carry four gallon cans of aviation fuel (two per man per trip) from the hangar, along and up the railway embankment and load them on to steel covered railway trucks which were like ovens inside. It was debatable which was worse. Having to carry two cans per trip over and over again, or having to work in the trucks stacking the cans. One of the lads thought up a crazy but rather daring idea. In the hangar were a number of empty wooden crates. One part of each crate featured a piece of softwood with a nail sticking out of each end. He took one of these without being noticed by the Jap guards and placed it in the long grass at the bottom of the railway embankment where the trucks were being loaded. With the nails pointing upwards it is easy to guess what was likely to happen. As every fourth or fifth can carrier took a rest in the long grass he placed his cans over the nails and then loaded the punctured cans on to the trucks. Needless to say these particular cans arrived at their destination 'sans' contents. Surprisingly there was never a murmur of complaint from the Japs. Uncanny!

We then resumed our crater filling duties but with additional pressure. We were now working seven days a week and had been for some time. As a result of the privation of our living accommodation dysentery and malaria became rife. I suffered a severe dose of malaria.

I would not wish this illness on my worst enemy and not wishing to appear alarmist it reached epidemic proportions in our camp. Without exaggeration some two hundred and fifty of the three hundred and odd inmates succumbed to the disease. The whole building became a hospital. Fortunately our work at the aerodrome was coming to an end and the much reduced workforce was able to cope with the demands of the Japs, although at the end of the working day many of our lads returned in a state of collapse only making it back with support from fitter colleagues. In my case, as the malaria advanced I became lost to reality with a sickening brain fever accompanied by intense shivering and involuntary teeth chattering. At one point I recall that my mental processes were confused to the extent that I believed I was traversing the same piece of roadway over and over again reaching a level where I would shout out loudly and incoherently. My pulse became so rapid it couldn't be counted and my head was splitting by the hammering of so many quinine tablets. Occasionally I would fall into normal deep sleep and waken to realise that all had lifted but my clothing stank from stale sweat.

The work on the airfield was completed and rather strangely we felt quite proud of what we had achieved in such a short space of time and with such primitive methods. We were keen not to give any indication of our pride to the Japs. The Mad Captain told WO Bardsley that tomorrow would be a holiday. '*All men Yasume*'. Quite a change from our normal routine. Washing and cleaning was the order of the day by those capable. Suddenly we were alerted by the drone of aircraft engines. In the sky were a number of Japanese twin- engine medium bombers with bomb doors open revealing twin rows of bombs. They passed low over us and eventually landed on the airfield. This was obviously the reason for 'Yasume'. Our immediate reaction to their arrival was 'Are they going to operate from here?' If so we could be right in the target area should the Allies attempt a reprisal bombing. From that day forward, and without fail, at six o'clock each morning the engines of these planes would be started up and taken up to peak revs without actually taking off.

So far I have probably given the impression that our gang was made up of mainly Ground Crew and Admin people. Not the case. Amongst us were a number of Air Crew made up mainly of Pilot Officer, Flight Lieutenant and Squadron Leader rank. After a fairly successful war in the Middle East their squadron (84 Squadron) was transferred, all too late, to the Far East. They were to be equipped with Hawker Hurricane fighters and it was planned that the ship which they joined would be carrying new 'crated' Hurricanes. However, the Japs had different ideas. The ship was attacked and its contents consigned to the depths of the Indian Ocean to the eternal care of Davy Jones. I believe that some of these pilots did get the opportunity to fly in anger from bases in Java but in unfamiliar planes and, I regret to say, with little success. Now pilots are a species all of their own. Our pilots were no different probably due to their earlier wartime experience. Whilst we were in this abominable accommodation they hatched out an escape plan. It was to go something like this –

On a pre-arranged day they would break out (no difficulty in that) in the early morning just before the Japs began the revving up process. They would then skirt the south side of the airfield and whilst the engines were still running over -power the ground crew and simply take off. Their destination would be Australia. The main risk they envisaged was whether the planes were fully fuelled which would determine their flying range.

The plan was deadly serious. Not a figment of wild imagination. One of the pilots quite casually told a New Zealand Stores Admin Officer called Flying Officer Bruce Paxton of their now advanced plan. He went into a terrific rage and vetoed the whole plan. The fact that some of the pilots outranked Paxton didn't seem to matter. He cited two very good reasons why the enterprise should not take place. 1 If six or eight planes approached the north coast of Australia clearly displaying Jap insignia they would most probably be blasted out of the sky and 2 Even if successful the Japs would take reprisal action by slaughtering so many of us unfortunates left behind. So much for that!

On 23 May 1942 we were on the move yet again. The general consensus was that wherever it is it will be an improvement on what we have endured so far. We travelled by train in an easterly direction. The journey was hot but uneventful and we eventually arrived at Surabaya the second largest city on Java. Alighting from the train at Surabaya we quickly realised that the number of Jap guards had increased significantly. Probably because the city environment could facilitate escape and make hiding much easier. We marched through the streets arriving at a large compound called 'Jaarmarkt' (translated as yearly market). It had a large exhibition area which had been turned into a prison camp. Our journey had taken about twelve hours and had sapped the strength of us malaria graduates. As it was now dark it was difficult to assess the area accurately but it did seem much different from anything experienced so far. Quite forbidding. We were beaten into line by rifle butts and bamboo poles. Even though it was dark there was to be a kit inspection. The Japs took great delight in rummaging through our meagre personal belongings. They would stick bayonets into bed rolls and pillows and also had a penchant for collecting photos of prisoner's wives and girlfriends. These photos would mean nothing to a Jap soldier. In my case I did have a photo of a girl called Gladys Davies. It was not that important to me but it is worth relating how it came to be in my possession. On that memorable day of enlistment at Padgate (18 June 1940) when I received my first uniform, I found in one of the pockets a short note which said '*If any young man should find this note, think of the girl who made this coat*'. This was followed by her name and address which was 42 Hows Street, Kingsland Road, East London. We had corresponded up to the time of my overseas draft and had exchanged photographs. The photo was removed from my possessions but what for? I know that East London received considerable attention by the Luftwaffe and I often wonder what happened to her and where she is now.

I mentioned earlier 'Tenko', the counting of prisoners. It rarely went smoothly and often ended in confusion. It soon became obvious that the average Jap soldier had never mastered arithmetic. Here was another example. After being counted for the umpteenth time it began to rain quite heavily and before we were dismissed our already opened belongings were now wet through. There was then a mad dash to get the best bed space. These were located in bamboo constructed buildings and are constructed from 'Bali-Bali' which is made by splitting lengths of bamboo down one side and then cracking it open until it is flat. It is then tied to a base frame about two feet above ground level by rattan thongs. Each construction could extend for some twenty or thirty feet thus creating a form of communal bed. Each individual had about about twenty seven inches width, the boundaries of which quite frequently led to disputes. Bali-Bali provided a perfect breeding ground for bugs and cockroaches which we were soon to find out. Shortly afterwards we were called back to the centre of the camp by unfamiliar shouts of '*Come and get it*'. On arrival we saw a fairly hefty Dutchman standing behind a large tub of soup. Our greeting went something like this '*Ve hear too late dat you is coming. Ve are sorry dat diss is all ve have. Ve have no time to cook da rice and der is no meat. Hope you like da soup. Diss is nothing. Wait until tomorrow when ve have da proper soup. Diss is not bad place. In da morning rice pap or bread roll. In da midday boiled rice. In da night after vork meat soup and steamed rice. Not bad. Name of da camp Jaarmarkt. Vork plenty, food plenty. Japanese bastards but der is no need to vorry. Ve hear it is pretty certain da Japs losing da var. Maybe all over in two veeks*'. Super-optimist.

Tenko was at seven the following morning. We saw the place in daylight for the first time. It appeared totally different from the night before. We joined about four thousand others on the square. They were of every nationality. Chinese, Ambonese, Javanese, Dutch, Canadian, American and British. A Jap sergeant stood on a high wooden platform at the front. He shouted out a command in Japanese. This meant we had to take off our hats and bow to the rising sun which was just appearing over the nearby roof tops. He then shouted another command which meant we had to put our hats back on. We were then introduced to 'Radio Taiso' which provided a daily broadcast aimed at factory workers. This meant that they had to down tools and perform ten minutes of physical exercise. We were required to do the same and Jap soldiers would patrol to see that we were extending ourselves correctly. Slackers would be prodded with sharp sticks and every now and then someone would break wind.

After completing our 'exercises' the senior Dutch Officer told us to stay behind where we were addressed by a Japanese Disciplinary Sergeant. Using three interpreters he impressed upon us several times that we had been 'spared' our lives by kind permission of the Emperor. He mentioned many things. We would be protected from the natives outside. We should never attempt to escape. In the event of a successful escape then wives and families of Dutchmen or ten ordinary prisoners would be shot. We had to bow to the rising sun each morning and also bow or salute every Japanese Officer and soldier and many more things. One in particular caused much amusement amongst us (when it shouldn't). He said 'No singing allowed'. A lot of us thought he meant 'No singing aloud'. How would they know if we were complying?

At each corner of the camp there was a sentry tower each with two sentries. We had to bow to these too. We were issued with small cloth numbers which had to be attached to our clothing by a safety pin. These were in different colours, the colour indicating the nationality of the wearer. White indicated Dutch. Green indicated

Native Dutch and red indicated British or American. This had a surprising spin-off. Rumours quite frequently circulated on the grapevine that the wearers of certain numbers were Jap informers arousing a lot of suspicion and causing you to look at the number before the face. As an example, I noticed that a Dutchman was frequently seen hanging about the British barracks. I made a note of his number. I will mention the outcome later.

Working parties were required daily. Every morning Jap soldiers would arrive to collect POW Working Parties. The work was usually of a very heavy nature either at the oil refinery, on the docks or the aerodrome. It didn't seem to matter whether it was work of military importance or not. The more knowledgeable amongst us explained that under the Geneva Convention employment of POWs in this way was forbidden. Japan had signed the Convention but hadn't ratified it so they didn't feel bound by its conditions. In the early days of captivity submissions by POWs to the Japanese guards relating to this were simply ignored. Later in 1942 the International Red Cross urged compliance but the answer from the Japs was '*As much as possible*'. In November 1942 conditions worsened. General Immamura Hitoschi of the 16th Army was succeeded by Lieutenant General Harada Kumakichi. Tokyo instructed him to act more firmly. New stricter orders for POWs were drafted by Major General Maruyama Masao. This was their response to '*As much as possible*'.

As POW working parties returned to camp each evening they regularly told stories of mistreatment and actual beatings for no apparent reason. According to the Japanese Code a POW was a vanquished person (in

Japanese a 'Furyo') and was assimilated with the lowest grade of their society. In other words he was a 'Hinin' (slave) and could be treated as wished. This became part of the Jap soldier's psyche allowing him to use both mental and physical abuse in a most sadistic manner. They were the conquerors so could behave as they wished. They applied the same attitude to the native Indonesians.

I then had a recurrence of my malaria and felt quite unwell. I was classified as Sick in Quarters (SIQ) when most men were out at work. At this time I saw my Dutch friend hanging about the British Quarters again. I was still guessing as to his motive? Whilst I was SIQ the Japs announced at Tenko that they had achieved several successes. Without foundation the Dutch always made counter claims. Whichever was correct the Jap victories always seemed to provide benefits in the strangest of ways and on this occasion they announced that the following day the gates of the camp would be thrown open to allow civilian visitors. My illness prevented my attendance but Bill Faulder went and told me later what went on. At two thirty in the afternoon the gates opened to a sea of anxious faces. They were clutching heavy baskets of food including home- made cakes. A bullock cart arrived laden with bananas, sweet potatoes, tinned food and several other items. The reunion, greetings and giving of presents continued until six o'clock when all the visitors were required to leave and the gates closed. That evening my malaria made sleep difficult and in the early hours all other inmates were sound asleep. However, the silence was frequently interrupted by the 'breaking of wind' by those who had gorged themselves that afternoon and as the night progressed the flatulence seemed to get louder and louder and sounded like the woodwind section of a thirty two piece orchestra.

On 5 September we were on the move again. Just a short move about a mile away to the HBS School. Formerly a Dutch High School known locally as The Lyceum. It was well appointed and like most schools had a main courtyard, an assembly hall and a playing field. Just before leaving The Jaarmarkt we had been ordered by the Camp Commander to organise a football match. It was to be an International match between England and Holland and was to be played at The Jaarmarkt. What we didn't realise was that the wall opposite our billet was in fact the boundary wall of an adjoining football stadium. This was where the match was to be played. To facilitate entry a whole section of wall was removed. This was to provide the answer to my suspicions regarding the Dutch man who was always hanging around this area. He was meeting his former house boy who, on a pre-arranged basis, say every two days, would bring chocolate, sugar, butter and cigarettes for his former boss and throw them over the wall for his collection. Nothing to worry about! As for the football match, I can't remember the exact score but England won. This was thanks to our centre forward, a chap called Bombardier Hands. Even though he was playing barefoot he could strike a ball with more force than most modern day footballers equipped with the latest footwear. I recall that one of his shots was so fierce that it dislocated the Dutch goalkeeper's finger.

At the HBS Bill Faulder and I got split up. We were still in contact but our bed spaces were in different parts of the school. Tenko took place on the playing field and like all others was a shambles. But, you will remember the monkey that amused on the train journey from Cilacap to Yogyakarta, well here he was and by now he was quite tame. During Tenko he would sit quietly on the crossbar of one of the goals. This may be difficult to believe but as a Jap guard approached it would cry like a baby and if it sensed the approach would make a dash for a nearby row of poplar like trees and climb to the very top. There it would remain keeping a close watch on the Tenko and once it knew that the count was over would descend rapidly and with uncanny accuracy find its 'handler' out of the hundreds of POW's present.

At this camp we had two very good RAF Medical Officers. Squadron Leader McCarthy and Flight Lieutenant Tierney. Both were Irish. They worked under considerable difficulty. The main problem was dysentery. A fly-borne disease which loosens the bowel action to the point of internal bleeding. Prevention rather than cure was insisted upon. As a result the Japanese C.O. directed that all POW's must have their heads shaved. Some POWs resisted but there were to be no exceptions and in our heart of hearts we knew it was a good idea as it should help control head-lice which was an ongoing problem amongst POWs. An American Airforce man called Corkindale (nicknamed Corky) sought a compromise. He asked the camp barber to leave the initials US in slightly longer hair on the top of his head. The rule was that if your hair could be held between thumb and index finger it was too long. The Jap guards enforced this religiously.

My new bed space was in the assembly hall where I slept next to a clean looking Irishman called Corporal 'Paddy' Semple, RAF. We became firm friends except that he kept pestering me for cigarettes. From time to time the Japs would find bulk supplies of locally made cigarettes and would distribute them to the POWs at the rate of ten per man. I didn't smoke. Paddy did. When he had smoked all of his he would ask me (although he knew my answer), *'Have you still got those fags?'* 'Yes'. *'Will you sell them?'* 'No, not until the price goes up'. *'You're a tight bugger'*. I always held them until the price would allow me to purchase black market sugar which was more important to me than cigarettes. The scarcity and poor quality of the rations meant that by mid- afternoon hunger would take over resulting in diz-ziness, a faint feeling and general weakness. This was particularly critical if you were on an outside working party. In camp a spoonful (yes, just one spoonful) worked as a miracle cure and alleviated the suffering almost immediately.

Deaths began to occur, mostly from dysentery and malnutrition. To supplement the meagre diet we were permitted to light open fires and cook concoctions of all kinds. This led to the creation of 'Kongsies' a Chinese word which singularly means 'family'. In camp, three or more men would pool their resources in an attempt to sustain each other whenever the need arose. For instance if one became ill the others would do his washing and so on. Those who went out working had a chance to buy some extras which would be brought back to camp and shared amongst their Kongsie members. The funds for such ventures were obtained by selling textiles and other valuables to the locals.

At the front of the Assembly Hall there was a gravel driveway leading to the entrance doors. The driveway followed a semi-circular route around a patch of grass in the centre of which was a mature palm tree. The trunk of the tree bristled with porcupine like spikes and its base was riddled with ants. One morning we awoke to see two native Javanese tied back to back to the tree with wire. It was only seven o'clock and we couldn't comprehend what was happening. Two short, muscular Jap soldiers were taking it in turns to run across the grass, jump at the two men and then punch them violently under their hearts. The two men were gasping for breath and only their bonds prevented them from falling forwards. Paddy and me had an unrestricted view of what was happening but still couldn't understand why? The Guardhouse was situated to the left of the palm tree and from time to time the Jap guards would get up and stub their cigarettes out on the foreheads or chests of the two men. One guard took great delight in pushing a piece of wire up the noses of the two men causing their heads to jerk backwards violently. Eventually one of the men collapsed and fell forward only to be suspended by the thongs holding his wrists together. One of the guards then gave him a vicious punch in the face and undid the wire so that he fell motionless to the ground. A Jap Sergeant then arrived and questioned the two men. They couldn't speak. Only nod their heads. The questioning lasted for another twenty minutes and it was apparent that the answers the Japs were looking for weren't forthcoming so the torture continued. Eventually the two were released and one of the guards gave each of them a white bread roll. Locals were not accustomed to eating anything made from white flour. Boldly they tried to eat but found it difficult as their lips and tongues were probably so swollen after their terrible ordeal. We learnt later that they were

Dutch Colonial Soldiers and were accused of trying to escape. They obviously spoke Malay and knowing that the Japs spoke little or no Malay or if they did, it was their own version of Malay, which was difficult to understand, the two men would find it impossible to follow the Jap questioning adding to the Japs anger and impatience. Having witnessed this event I was glad that I had made an attempt to learn Malay whilst on board the troopship and in Malaya itself. So even after all these years I think the conversation may have gone something like this - The native men '*Roti tidah nasi-makanan*'. (Bread no, we eat rice). The Jap Guard pointing towards us '*Roti bagus, samoa Ingerris makan roti*'. (Bread is good, look all the English eat bread). To our great surprise and indeed pleasure the Jap Sergeant allowed Flight Lieutenant Tierney to attend them. He dressed their cuts and abrasions but the taller of the two natives had a gaping wound between his neck and his shoulder. We didn't think he had acquired this whilst we were watching. The MO wanted to take him to his surgery but the Jap Sergeant wouldn't allow this and promptly berated the MO. There then followed further torture. The two men were made to hold a concrete slab at arms-length above their heads. The penalty for lowering or dropping the slab was to be further kicked or punched. There then followed a perfect example of Japanese tactics when dealing with prisoners. The two men were allowed to put down the slabs and a Jap guard then gave each man a cigarette and even lit it for them. This alternating torture regime went on for six days. I will not detail the further ill treatment except to mention the forced drinking of salt water which in itself is an emetic.

In the meantime a bamboo cage had been built on the far side of the playing field. The cage was only some two feet six inches high and its roof was constructed of corrugated metal sheets which served to increase the inside temperature considerably when the sun shone (which it frequently did). The two men were taken to the cage, thrown in and tied securely. It was impossible for them to sit up without bending their head forward. We saw them during every Tenko and heard them being beaten frequently.

Our first Christmas in captivity was fast approaching but the torture of the two natives which most of us had witnessed had served to sap our morale which in all honesty is probably what the Japs wanted. To combat this we asked for and were granted permission to hold a concert on the playing field. Some resourceful prisoner 'located' a dartboard so it was decided that a darts competition would form part of the concert. We were divided into teams representing our home county. This created a lot of interest and each game drew lots of spectators. Cumberland, my home county, was always going to struggle to provide a team as there were so few of us. However, we did manage to raise a team and even after all these years I can recall its members. J Sowerby from Thursby was captain and other team members were J Williamson from Carlisle, L Cranston from Bransty, J Tinnion from Longtown, T Knight from Durdar, Bill Faulder from Penrith and me. We had to co-opt another member to make up the team of eight. Needless to say we finished last. With the approach of Christmas we were constantly looking out for better 'fare'. Those going out on working parties did their best to bring back any extras that they could locate. One speciality was Katchang Idjoe a kind of small tropical pea. The Medical Orderlies were pleased as this was a rich source of Vitamin C. In addition the Japs gave us permission to purchase one duck egg each per day. This was a welcome change so Christmas may not be so bad after all.

Despite all the hardships there were certain optimists amongst the POWs who were frequently forecasting *'It's OK, we'll be out in three weeks'*. There was no apparent basis for these comments and it was difficult to identify their motives. Obviously their forecasts never reached fruition so it was best to regard them with suspicion and check the credibility of each one. Rumours were rife, not least those relating to impending moves. More often than not these turned out to be true. So it was with the latest rumour. We were on the move yet again. It was 17 December, just eight days before Christmas. No transport this time. A forced march. We had no idea of the distance. It turned out to be just five miles. But five gruelling miles which took us outside the city boundary into open countryside. This should have been refreshing but the heat was oppressive and it became a struggle for the weakest amongst us. The column got longer and longer much to the annoyance of the Jap Guards. Some POWs could not even maintain the slowest pace and actually collapsed. We eventually reached our destination, the stragglers being delivered by truck. It was a former Dutch Naval Shore Station called 'Darmo' and had been converted into a prison camp. It had an arched entrance and a compound which was circled by whitewashed barrack rooms. Compared with the Jaarmarkt and Lyceum it looked quite clean and civilised. Lush green grass covered the square but this was out of bounds except for the customary kit search. The square was bordered by tarmac roads. This is where Tenko took place. We were required to form up in four lines with each line comprising twenty five men making one hundred per section. Simple to count, eh? No not really and it was always an interesting and amusing event. Those in the front line, on the command 'Bango' meaning 'number' in English, were required to count off in Japanese. So knowing how reluctant us Brits are to learn a foreign language meant that no-one wanted to be in the front line. The Bango was meant to go like this – *Ichi, Ni, San, Shi, Go, Roku, Shichi, Hachi, Kyu, Ju (ten)* thus *eleven is Ju-ichi, twelve is Ju-ni* and so on. Twenty is *Ni-ju* with the tens always placed before the units. So the last man on the front rank is *Ni-ju-go* which when pronounced sounds like 'need you go' in English making it easy to remember. All the Jap guards required was for the numbers to be shouted out sharp and loud (just like they speak themselves) and as long as they heard 'Ichi' from the first man and Ni-ju-go from the last man they were happy. The rest of the front row shouted out all manner of things which were never queried by the Japs so how accurate each 'Tenko' was remains a matter of conjecture.

Here, we had Radio Taiso again but no early morning sun worship. The food was well cooked and the Commandant quite co-operative so we all felt better, both physically and mentally. There was no outside work as such but small working parties were allowed to go outside to cultivate vegetable gardens for our own use. The Commandant wanted us to become self- sufficient within a given time. Everyone entered into this task enthusiastically and by Christmas Day most of us were feeling the benefit of the exercise, the open air and the sunshine. To everyone's surprise the Commandant presented each of us with a Christmas gift of a new shirt. We were starting to become suspicious as to his motives but, conversely, some were starting to think our enemy isn't so bad after all. Christmas Lunch was rice with soup and was quite acceptable. So Christmas wasn't too bad after all. A few days later the Commandant allowed us to write and send our first post-card home. The limit was to use two set phrases and twenty five words of your own. I tried to include a hidden message in mine. I said *'The food is good, just like Station View'*. The reader will not be aware but Station View was the local Poor Law Institute in Penrith, more commonly known as 'The Workhouse'. A few days later we were all ordered to file singly through the Jap Admin Office where our fingerprints were taken. I never did discover the reason why?

Just as we were becoming acclimatised to our new relaxed atmosphere the camp rumour machine reared its ugly head again. Another move? Once again it turned out to be true. So on 10 January 1943 we were one the move yet again only twenty four days after arriving at Darmo. We were sure that this almost constant moving was a deliberate tactic by the Japs to try and unsettle us and break our morale as there was no obvious reason why we were being moved so frequently. Most of us would have preferred to stay in one place, irrespective of what conditions prevailed and no matter how long we were to be guests of The Emperor. The frequent packing, unpacking, tying and untying of bed rolls and bed mats was most annoying and taking its toll on us.

We marched re-tracing the route we had used to arrive at Darmo. Amongst our group were Dutchmen who had previously lived in Surabaya and as we approached the outskirts there was commentary from them as to where we might be heading. Not The Lyceum as we were advised that we had passed beyond that area. I calculated that we had been on the march for over three hours when suddenly we came upon The Jaarmarkt. It came as a surprise as we had approached from a different direction. We entered to the disappointment of everyone. This had been our home from 23 May to 5 September and wasn't particularly welcoming. We were counted and searched yet again. This was followed by an indoctrination lecture by the Jap Commandant who kept referring to 'The Jaarmarkt Spirit' which fell on deaf ears as we hadn't a clue what he was talking about. One POW was heard to exclaim 'Ridiculous, abso-bloody-lutley ridiculous'. It would be fair to say that swearing was commonplace amongst the men and could be much worse than the example just quoted. It was seen as a safety valve for the anger and frustration which was commonplace and was never challenged.

This time we were housed on the opposite side of the exhibition ground in the tattered remnants of bamboo warrens formerly occupied by the Chinese. Down each side were long rows of 'bali-bali' with an earth corridor running up the centre. There was certainly a touch of the dèja vu which could have been demoralising as the conditions here compared most unfavourably to those at Darmo. But they were better than The Lyceum. There was more room and here we had a good, well equipped sick bay. The two natives who had been so cruelly tortured at The Lyceum had been brought and were now locked in underground cells. Our billet was close to the toilet block which could be an advantage if you had to make a rapid visit (which was not uncommon) but this was far outweighed by the disgusting smell which was quite nauseating in the tropical heat.

Working parties by the dozen left the camp each morning. These were closely supervised by the Japs and often arguments would break out between Jap and POW over the slightest matter. The language barrier inevitably led to the argument becoming more heated and the Jap taking his frustration out on the POW by giving him a severe beating. All of which were completely unnecessary and avoidable. Quite often the Jap guards would provoke the POWs. I recall two incidents on the same day. We were on an outside working party at Surabaya Airport (now a Jap Air Force Station). Our job was to build gun emplacements around the airport perimeter. Only one Jap guard was present and he kept interrupting saying in his best Malay '*Tojo bagoose, Churchill tidah bagoose*'. 'Tojo (the Japanese Prime Minister) is a good man, Churchill a bad one'. Some amongst us dared to reply indicating the opposite. This caused the Jap to 'boil' inside resulting in him lashing out with his rifle butt. For lunch we had to march around the corner from where we were working. On this occasion our Officer in Charge was an RAF Pilot Officer of advancing years. He was one of the co-opted admin men and was very quietly spoken. We were counted and searched and told to form up by the Jap guard and then our Officer in Charge said in almost inaudible tones '*Quick March*'. The Jap went berserk. He called us back and by example showed us how it should really be done by shouting out the command in a loud, rasping voice. He then indicated that our OIC should do it again properly. This time the OIC called on his best strengths (completely against his nature) and shouted out loudly '*Attention. Right turn. Bugger off and get your lunch*'. The guard was delighted.

The second interesting event was most rewarding for us. Lunch turned out to be thin watery vegetable soup. After the soup we were each given a half Dixie of green leaf tea and a thirty minute '*Yasume*'. As we were enjoying our rest the Jap Guard who had been aggressive towards us all morning and obviously 'fancied' himself pointed to one of our lads, a Corporal Almond, and said '*You, me Ju-jitsu-ka*'. What the Jap didn't know was that Corporal Almond was a physical training NCO and an exponent in nothing less than Ju-Jitsu. He was still in good bodily shape (probably why the Jap picked on him) and accepted the Jap's challenge. Almond then demonstrated his prowess and gave the Jap a lesson in Ju-Jitsu. As we resumed after lunch the Jap guard was replaced and, believe it or not, he was then given another thrashing by his section guards.

Relating this occurrence reminds me of 'Bushido'. Some readers may be familiar with the word. Translated literally it means 'The way of the warrior' and is based on Samurai life. It can be summarised as 'honour till death' and has become the martial code of Japan. This code raised martial conduct to the level of a culture and almost a religion to millions of Japanese males. So defeat was seen as humiliation and was so powerful that death was often seen as preferable. Hence, kamikaze pilots and suicide squads. This certainly influenced the attitude of the Jap guards to POWs who, having surrendered, were regarded as the lowest of the low and could be treated accordingly. The horrendous cruelty inflicted by the 'Kempetai', the Japanese Secret Police, exemplifies this perfectly. I mentioned earlier the refusal of the Japanese to ratify the Geneva Convention relating to the treatment of prisoners and can now understand why? It would have contradicted the Bushido Code!

The first anniversary of capture went by almost unnoticed. So much for *'It'll be all over in three weeks'*. Where were these optimists now? The year in captivity was taking its toll. We had been dominated, slave driven, isolated from any form of civilisation (apart from, perhaps 'Darmo') and starved of any comfort. Our bodies had slowly adapted to the poor diet but any physical reserves had been used up and mentally it was hard to stay strong. Illness was rife, particularly dysentry and malaria and was beginning to undermine any power of resistance. As a humorous aside to this, an RAF POW called Ashworth introduced his own form of National Health Insurance. Those POWs who went out to work were paid two pence per day by the Japs. On pay day the workers paid Ashworth one penny per day. If they were unable to work for three days or more he would 'pay out' the same as if they had worked. It was doomed to failure as the incidence of sickness increased dramatically.

At this point I was stricken with double pneumonia. I was to be SIQ as the sick bay was full. Bill Faulder was very good and tended to most of my needs. The MO was Flight Lieutenant Braithwaite (our MO back in KL). He gave me repeated M and B tablets (a rarity) but my condition did not respond. I recall lying there in

considerable pain when the loudspeaker would play
'*Come back to Sorrento*'. I didn't know the song then
but every time I hear it now my mind instantly flashes
back to that time in sick bay at the Jaarmarkt. Rumours
of another move were circulating which I found distressing given my present state of health.

On the morning of 13 April Doc Braithwaite told me
that I was down for a move. Unfortunately Bill Faulder
wasn't. My move was to take place in the early evening.
A number of Jap trucks arrived in camp. I was lifted on
to a bamboo stretcher and carried down to the square.
All I had was a pack, a bed mat and one bed sheet. I said
goodbye to Bill and was then loaded into one of the
trucks along with three other stretchered POWs. We
travelled to the railway station where I was transferred
to a waiting train. By this time it was dark and I was
pleased that the move wasn't taking place in the heat of
the day. I had no sense of direction of travel but could
work out our speed from the noise of the train. It was
pitch black inside the train. I sensed that there were
others present but didn't know how many. One thing
that did change was the temperature inside the train. It
had become considerably cooler meaning that we may
have climbed to a higher level. The single bed sheet
wasn't much use to combat the cold and I recall a
feeling of self-pity encroaching. '*How long had I been in
captivity?*' '*How long is it since I left home?*' This
caused me to reflect on my last visit home whilst on
embarkation leave. I purposely wish to record here
something that I have never spoken about or written
about in all the intervening years.

I have never been very good at 'Good Byes' as I find
the emotions and sentiments difficult to deal with. To

offset this, on the second day of my leave, I said to my mother '*When I go I want to walk out as if I'm just going to work and when I come back I would like to arrive as if I had just returned from work*'. This was agreed without discussion. The next day we were having a morning cup of tea when without hesitation we embraced each other, not a word was said and we both cried. That spoke more than any words ever could. That moment will live in my mind until I die. Why was I thinking it now in this smelly rail van?

The train came to a halt and the doors opened to reveal the half- light of breaking dawn. The place was called Cimahi. I'd never heard of it. It was cold and I couldn't control my shivers. I was loaded into a waiting lorry. Mercifully it was only a short trip as we soon arrived at a clean looking building. It was a proper hospital. It turned out that this was the only hospital on Java, an island as big as Britain, which had been reserved solely for POWs. I've mentioned previously the possibility of divine intervention on my part. This was surely another example. I couldn't put the arrival at a properly functioning hospital down to luck. In that smelly rail van I was in the depths of despair, feeling particularly unwell and not knowing what was to come. Now my spirits had lifted almost to the point of elation and as it turned out Cimahi hospital was to play a significant role in my recovery to reasonable health.

The hospital had four detached wards, an operating theatre, an X-ray department and a pharmacy. It was obviously a legacy to the Japs from the Dutch Army. The paths connecting the various departments were covered to provide protection from the sun and rain. I was placed in Ward 4. A man in Dutch Army green uniform approached. His peaked hat had the customary orange button in the centre. He was on crutches and spoke to me. Here I got the surprise of my life. He said in broad Cumberland dialect *'Where's thoo cum fray?'* I replied *'It must be somewhere near thee, I cum fray Peereth'*. He said *'Dun't mention Peereth to me, it was a Peereth gadji (man) who put me in here'*. He was an army despatch rider called Turnbull who hailed from Mealsgate. During 'action' the Field Artillery were moving under the cover of darkness (and it does get very dark in the tropics) and being patrolled from end to end by two despatch riders. In the darkness they collided 'head-on'. Turnbull was one of the despatch riders and the other was a man called Tommy Jackson (fray Peereth) but I can't say I knew him.

The hospital was staffed entirely by Dutch Army personnel. The Japs were nowhere to be seen. Probably due to their intense fear of catching even the common cold. A welcome factor. A Japanese Army doctor was in overall charge of the hospital but he was rarely seen. Wards 2 and 4 were occupied by British POWs. Wards 1 and 3 by Dutch POWs. I remained in Ward 4 where I met a man called Bill Griffiths. He was from Blackburn, Lancashire. Bill had been taken prisoner and had been sent out on working parties as usual. He was working at Bandung Aerodrome dismantling former Dutch Anti-Aircraft gun emplacements. Unknown to the working party the gun emplacements had been booby trapped by placing live hand grenades on the camouflage netting. As the netting was pulled away the grenades exploded. Bill was blinded and lost both hands. In the next bed to Bill was a man called Gatley. He had been performing a similar task to Bill and suffered the same consequences.

He too was blind and had shrapnel wounds to his face and chest. Apparently when Bill was made aware of his injuries by the medics he pleaded with them to end his life. Obviously their moral and professional codes did not allow this and their decision was Britain's gain. After a spell at an artificial limb centre Bill went to St Dunstan's and ultimately joined that very worthwhile organisation and has given them loyal and dedicated service. He appeared on the TV programme '*This is your life*' and was awarded the MBE on the same day as Princess Anne made our Queen a grandmother for the first time. He was ever present at the Armistice Parade at the Cenotaph marching proudly with the St Dunstan's contingent. I had the pleasure of meeting Bill at a Far East Prisoner of War re-union at Blackpool in the 1960's and again in Penrith when he gave a talk to Penrith British Legion. Bill passed away on 20 July 2012 aged 92 years.

The facilities at the hospital together with the better climate (the hospital was about 2,300 feet above sea level) was conducive to improved health and I soon felt much better. When I was at the Jaarmarkt I possessed only one pair of well- worn shoes and a pair of own make 'Klompers' (taken from the Dutch word Klompen meaning wooden clogs). These were fashioned from softwood into a shaped sole with a webbing strap attached over the instep and just behind the toes. I favoured these over shoes as I had developed the 'mother and father' of ingrowing toe nails on both big toes making shoes painful to wear. In camp the MO tried to alleviate the pain by packing the offending areas with copper sulphate crystals. This had a cauterising effect but did not provide a cure. At the hospital the Doctors became aware of this condition and as my pneumonia began to improve they decided that they should operate. I was more than agreeable and on the day walked to theatre. Two Dutch doctors were waiting. I climbed on to the operating table and my wrists and ankles were secured in straps. Rather like mediaeval torture procedure. I was given an anaesthetic by injection behind each toe nail. This in itself was painful. At intervals they pricked each toe and asked me if I could feel it. In every case I said most definitely that I could. The two doctors talked to each other within earshot. I had a basic understanding of Dutch and heard one say *'Het pijnverdovend ben oud'* (The anaesthetic is very old). The other replied *'Wij moet even proberen'* (We must try). Not very re-assuring. Without going into exact detail let me say that the operation was completed and I felt every part of it. I was then returned to Ward 2 with both toes heavily bandaged and both throbbing in unison with my heart. I hardly slept that night because of the pain and was beginning to subscribe to the view that my toes would have been better left alone. When the bandages were removed I saw that both nails had been removed. Eventually the left nail returned but the right one chose not to.

By now I had become accustomed to the 'good life' in Cimahi hospital but realised that it had achieved its aim by getting me better so was anticipating discharge quite soon. Then, as if by fate, my malaria returned. I was given intravenous injections, which I certainly wouldn't have received back in camp, and was quickly restored to normal. I was discharged on 2 June and walked to a new camp in Cimahi. I was given a bed space but I didn't know a soul. What a disappointment.

I quickly realised that the camp was populated almost entirely by Royal Artillerymen. The Billet Commander was a Company Sergeant Major Hunt. He was fairly typical of the 'regular' serviceman. A rather pasty faced individual, covered in tattoos and a bullying approach to POWs. One of his fellow POWs, a Gunner Birmingham confided in me that Hunt was full of confidence when dealing with his fellow POWs but was scared to death of the Japs. Birmingham was up to no good. Whenever a Jap guard entered the barracks the Officer in Charge was required to call out *'Kiotsuke'* and *'Kiree'* and all those present had to stand to attention and bow. In any given day this could happen several times and failure to comply usually resulted in a beating. On this particular day Birmingham told all the occupants, except Hunt, of his plan. He entered the barracks 'chuntering' just like a Jap guard. As we all stood to attention and bowed Hunt disappeared out of the open window. We all shouted after him *'Where are you going?'* I remained at Cimahi for only two days. On 4 June I was moved to nearby Bandung camp. I was more at home here. I was re-united with Bill Faulder which was a great pleasure and I also came across Tommy Jackson. He was the man 'fray Peereth' who had inflicted the injuries on Eric Turnbull who I met in Cimahi hospital. I hadn't met Tommy before but back home we met several times and reminisced about our time out here.

Bandung camp was a former Dutch Army camp and was ideally suited for its present purpose. Our Commander was Wing Commander Nicholls, RAF. The barracks formed four wings. Two were occupied by Dutch POWs, one by British POWs and one by Dutch

Colonial POWs. Each wing had its own canteen. Along one boundary was a street with semi-detached bungalows on each side. These had been the homes of former Dutch Officers and their families. In the camp sport and pastimes were encouraged. Tommy Jackson played baseball nearly every day and the British had turned the gym into a theatre. It had an orchestra pit, floodlights made from old car headlamps and curtains salvaged from the local cinema (POWs, particularly the British, were very resourceful). Some excellent revues and plays were presented. For example, I recall '*The Importance of being Earnest*' being performed. There was an army officer called Hugh Moxey and an RAF man called Clive Brett who had both been actors. Also there was a Flight Lieutenant from New Zealand (whose name escapes me) who was a scenic artist. So the performances were very professional and most enjoyable.

There was little interference from the Japs but they did mount an Anti-Dysentry Campaign. They issued a directive that every day each nationality had to catch a given quota of flies which had to be handed to the Japs at six o'clock each evening. Once again the resourcefulness of the British showed itself. They had a plan. The Chinese contingent in Barrack 4 were particularly good at catching flies and regularly exceeded their quota without difficulty. So it was arranged that they would continue catching until they had enough for the British to achieve their quota as well. We then 'bought' the flies and handed them over to the Japs at six o' clock. A case of '*No flies on the British!*' It was not unusual for a camp to have its own vocabulary where previously unknown words or phrases would be taken into daily use. One of these was the 'Lagi Queue'. 'Lagi' is the

Malay word for 'more'. At each mealtime we had to form a line to receive our food. Rice was dished out from a large wooden tub using a tin can which had been nailed to a stick. The rice would be served into your Dixie as the line moved along until all had been served. If there was still some rice left then a second line would form for a second serving until all the rice had gone. This second line became known as the 'Lagi Queue' and it soon became evident that it was always the same men who formed it for the simple reason that these same men were always at the front of the first line. So in the interest of fair play it was agreed that the camp nominal role would be used for the 'Lagi Queue'. The name of the last man to receive rice when it finally ran out would be noted and at the next 'Lagi Queue' the first in the queue would be the next man on the nominal role. This may sound trivial but the reader will by now be aware of the importance of food to a POW. It was the cause of many arguments so 'fair play' in its distribution was paramount. The system I have just described was accepted unanimously.

The Jap Commandant decreed that the camp should become self-sufficient (we had heard this before at Darmo) but this time it appeared serious. We were to rear and keep pigs and ducks and grow sweet potatoes. The POWs entered enthusiastically into the project. Soon there was fierce competition between the British and the Dutch and once again the British resourcefulness proved to be an advantage. I can say unequivocally that the British won in every aspect of the project. Each scheme had a Japanese guard to oversee it. Ours is worthy of description. Apart from the normal uniform, including the customary peaked cap, he wore puttees and special rubber footwear where the big toe is separated from the others. He wore horn rimmed specs with thick lenses and had peculiar legs. The knee joint was much lower than normal so his upper leg was much longer than the lower leg. Also he was very bow-legged. The Officer appointed to oversee the POWs side of each scheme was Lieutenant Colonel Laurens Van der Post. He was later to become Godfather to Prince William our future king. He was South African by birth but in the British Army. He spoke fluent Japanese and was able to influence our Jap on several issues.

We gave the Jap the nickname of 'Donald Duck'. He didn't realise this but answered willingly to the name 'Donaldo'. One of his enterprises was the construction of a large duck pond within the camp. This was stocked with a large number of ducks and a facility for egg laying was also provided. Donaldo also kept meticulous records on egg production. One day Donaldo told Lieutenant Colonel Van der Post that he had received a 'rocket' from his superiors because our egg production was falling daily. Donaldo then decided he must have a duck Tenko. Not an easy task, there were ducks everywhere. He scratched his head and muttered 'Mushkassi-na' (difficult-difficult) but he eventually decided he had the correct total. What he was not aware of (and neither was the Jap command) was that lots of the lads had their own ducks and in the dead of night they would visit the pond and replace the ducks with drakes. Thus his count was correct but it didn't account for the fewer eggs being produced. Eggs were of immense nutritional value so their production was encouraged by the MOs and they formed an important part of our daily diet.

British pig production was overseen by an RAF Sergeant called Giles. So he soon became known as 'Farmer Giles' which was then shortened to 'Farmer'. He was quite proud of his sobriquet and took his role seriously, so much so that he would frequently sit up all night with a sick pig in an attempt to get it better. Donaldo was the Jap in charge of our pig production. There now follows a short resumé on 'the facts of life'. One day 'Farmer' decided that one of his 'lady pigs' needed servicing by a 'gentleman pig'. Donaldo was consulted and said he would take charge of this. The 'gentleman pig' was an asset shared between the British and Dutch so had to be collected to perform his task. We then saw the bow-legged Donaldo wheeling a special type of barrow with the 'gentleman pig' inside. The two pigs were then introduced and in front of several interested POWs they 'performed'. After nature had taken its course the exertions of the 'gentleman pig' in the intense heat meant it was exhausted and steam was coming off it. To obviate any further transportation, Donaldo suggested to Farmer that if any other 'lady pigs' required 'servicing' then now was the time. The 'gentleman pig' obviously had other ideas as it promptly lay down and went to sleep. Donaldo exclaimed in broken Malay 'Orang pig tidah bagoose'. (Man pig no good).

About this time the Jap Command introduced a new system of prisoner identity numbers to replace the old cloth numbers issued way back at Jaarmarkt. The new ones, in addition to the number, would include two Japanese 'Kanji' characters indicating nationality and rank. These were made from cardboard so were not very durable. This resulted in a thriving industry producing aluminium name tags from dixies. The aluminium dixie was beaten flat and the name tag cut out to the required size. It was then engraved with the correct information, fitted with a safety pin and finally exposed to candle wax to fill in the engraving. My new number was 17230. A copy of my badge is reproduced below. It may be appropriate to point out that there are three types of Japanese characters. Kanji, Hirogana and Kata-Kana. The latter is the simplest. The characters on the badge are Kanji. The one on the left is 'Ei' for English. The one on the right is 'Hei' for soldier, thus 'Ei Hei' means English soldier. It is a little known but interesting fact that Kanji characters are more common to the Chinese than the Japanese so it is quite possible for Japanese and Chinese to write to each other in Kanji but couldn't use it to speak to each other. The Kanji characters on my badge would be interpreted by a Chinese person as 'Ing Ping' which is Chinese for English soldier.

It came to my attention that there were a couple of jobs available in the clothing repair shop for anyone who could operate a sewing machine. I applied along with an artilleryman from East Anglia and we were both successful. The gunner, whose name I can't remember, had suffered a serious injury to his left arm. It had been hit by shrapnel midway between shoulder and elbow. The bone had been shattered, losing about two inches, but muscle, nerves and sinews were still intact. The arm could well have been amputated but on this occasion the MOs had decided not to. Nature was now taking its course as the two ends of the shattered bone were starting to knit together. It turned out that he had received his wound in the Jap air raid on Cilacap and was one of the occupants of the lorry that we had witnessed pull up to ask the way to the hospital. He later introduced me to his colleague Gunner Flatman who was also from East Anglia and was also injured in the Jap air raid. He had lost his left arm just above the elbow. Our job at the repair shop was to salvage cloth from discarded clothing which was then used to carry out repairs, mainly to the backsides of trousers.

One day we were told that we were to be given the afternoon off which was quite surprising. So that afternoon I decided to sort out my belongings. Whilst I had disposed of my camera some time ago I did keep some photos and negatives. I was looking through these when suddenly the alarm bell started ringing. This meant we had to assemble on the square in double quick time. All my belongings were spread out on my bed so I gathered up all the photos and put them in a Players Flat 50 cigarette box, dived through the open window and hid the box in the sweet potato patch. We all assembled on the square, were counted and then marched up the road to the adjoining barracks where we had to hand pluck grass and weeds. The reason for this unusual occurrence soon became apparent. The Japs had conducted a thorough search of our barracks looking for weapons, radios and any other banned items. We were eventually marched back to our barracks and assembled on the square. We were ordered to place our hats on the ground and empty our pockets into them so that the Japs could see if we had anything we shouldn't have, such as too much money. I then realised that in my haste to get to the square I had put the photo negatives in my breast pocket. I panicked as I wasn't supposed to possess photos (remember the incident at the Jaarmarkt) so I pushed them down the back of my shorts and gripped them between my buttocks. Immediately to my right was the Senior MO, Wing Commander Coffey. As the Jap guard approached he saw that the MO had more money than the maximum allowed and promptly gave him a severe beating. He showed no interest in the contents of my hat and moved along. There then came the order to pick up our hats and belongings. I quickly realised that the human anatomy would not allow me to bend over without revealing my deceit so I asked the man on my left (I couldn't ask Coffey because he was still suffering the after effects of his beating) to do it for me. He was rather surprised but did it without question. The next command 'Right turn, quick march' proved rather difficult but, with bum nipped tight, I managed it without detection.

The clothes repair job soon came to an end but another opportunity arose. The senior British Officers were billeted in the semi-detached bungalows, formerly the homes of Dutch Officers and their families. A Batman was required. I will try anything once, applied and got the job. There were three officers to each bungalow. In my case there was Wing Commander Cave, Squadron Leader Page and Squadron Leader Alwyn. The latter was a long serving old sweat and quite a character. In the adjoining bungalow were three other officers two of which were Padres, all with Squadron Leader rank. One of the Padres was called Phillips. They were both great guys and very broad minded and contradicted the myth that all 'men of the cloth' are narrow minded old fuddy- duddys. In fact Padre Phillips took part in most of the concerts in the theatre and his rendition of 'Mad Dogs and Englishmen' was better than Noel Coward himself. I was one of three batmen. We slept in the outhouses at the rear of the bungalows. Our main job was to bring the meals from the camp kitchen and to wash up afterwards. At this point I took ill again. This time it was partial failure of my eyesight. Doc McCarthy told me that it was Avitaminosis which leads to Retrobulbar Neuritis. In layman's terms this is due to the poor nutritional value of the daily diet causing the nerves at the back of the eyes to fail. The treatment was most unusual. Doc McCarthy gave me a fever injection and I took to my bed sweating profusely and with a throbbing head. But it did the trick and I soon recovered.

Because my accommodation was now away from the main camp I thought it appropriate to get myself an 'interest' so I bought a black and white rabbit and built a hutch. I placed it near the back door of the bungalow. In the fullness of time Squadron Leader Alwyn (the old joker) suggested that my female rabbit should be introduced to a male rabbit just like Farmer Giles did with his lady pig. The only male rabbit was owned by Padre Phillips. Despite him being very broad minded I couldn't pluck up courage to ask him for the loan of his rabbit and for what purpose. Squadron Leader Alwyn said 'Leave it to me' and whilst the Padre was away at the main camp watching a baseball match he went and 'borrowed' the rabbit. It was introduced to my rabbit and in front of an audience of Senior RAF Officers performed admirably and was then returned to its own hutch. Now no-one knew with any accuracy the gestation period of a pregnant rabbit but we did know that after giving birth she must be left alone otherwise she will eat her young. Wing Commander Cave christened her Mrs Smith and every day all the Officers asked quite seriously about her current condition. There came a time when she started pulling off her own wool to make a nest and shortly afterwards gave birth to three babies. They grew rapidly.

The rumour machine was working overtime once again. Another move was in the offing. It turned out to be true. Unfortunately all pets had to be disposed of. I had become quite attached to Mrs Smith and her family and as hungry as we all were I couldn't bring myself to commit them to the pot. I sold them to the Dutch canteen. The lists of those who were to move were published. I was on the list, Bill Faulder wasn't, so once again we were to be split up. Whilst talking to Bill we recalled that those who had been left behind at the Jaarmarkt had eventually been transferred to a place called Haruku, a small island located to the south of the island of Ceram and close to the island of Ambon in an area known as the Moluccas just off West New Guinea. A journey of some 1,120 miles (1800 km). Over the intervening years I learnt that there were 2000 of them and that they were required to build an airstrip out of hewn solid rock. Deaths occurred regularly and Bill and I reflected that we were lucky not to be included in the Haruku draft. But where to next? It was Christmas Day 1943, just like any other day, when we were told that the move would be next day (Boxing Day). This caused me to reflect on my present position. Frequently, I used to look up at the sun and think that the very same sun would shortly be shining over Penrith, yet there was no way we could communicate with each other.

We left the next morning and the journey by train was unremarkable. We travelled west and eventually arrived in Batavia (now Jakarta). We marched to yet another Dutch barracks known as either The Tenth Battalion or The Cycle Camp, probably due to it formerly being the home of the Dutch Cycle Regiments. Being a former Dutch barracks it was similar to Bandung, the only difference being that it was within the city limits. Outside working parties were part of day to day life and I can recall two in particular. The first was to a place called St Vincentius, a former nunnery or something similar. We had to scrub acres of marble floor. Not too difficult when compared to previous tasks. We would all line up on our knees and reverse across the wide expanse of floor. At one end of the line of 'scrubbers' was a door to a store cupboard which was standing slightly ajar. The man on the end sneaked in for a 'recce'. He found a very old bulk tin containing a number of Fry's English Four Centre chocolate bars. It was quickly decided that the size of the tin would make it difficult to smuggle into camp so to ensure fair play, each of us in turn would go into the cupboard and consume ONE bar. The only drawback was that due to their age and probably the heat, it was impossible to remove the silver paper so, needs must, we just ate the lot. The second was a trip by lorry across the city to an industrial area. We entered the gas works where we saw a large conveyor discharging fine black coke ash and as it came off the conveyor it was forming a huge pyramid. One of the wags on board (imitating a Jap) said '*All men just move mountain, all go home*'. The lorry then did a 'U' turn and stopped at the pyramid. Next, and I'm sure you can guess, the Jap guard said '*All men off. All chunkels off.*' Then, pointing at the pyramid said '*All this road on rorry, take all to rairway all men go home*'. No more comment from the wag. Now sweating and shovelling fine coal dust don't exactly go together but it was one of those occasions when to look at each other caused fits of laughter. This in itself could be dangerous as the Jap may have thought we were laughing at him which would have resulted in a beating. Fortunately, this didn't happen but we must have been a pretty sight as we returned across the city with bloodshot eyes and pink tongues shining brightly through coal black faces.

It was here that I first thought about learning the Japanese language. I had become acquainted with two Chinese lads who were serving in the Dutch army when they were taken prisoner. They were really grand lads and when they make friends they are most sincere. One was called Tan Tjai Jam and the other Oei Boon Som. They, in turn, had another Chinese friend called Oei Kim Jan who had lived in Japan for some time and had a good working knowledge of day to day Japanese. I decided quickly that Japanese grammar was far too complicated to learn so committed to learning and compiling an enormous vocabulary. I compiled lots of notes with the help of Oei Kim Jan. One thought I had at this time was that this might help me eavesdrop on the Jap guards in the forlorn hope that I might learn something about the progress of the war. Unfortunately I never had the opportunity to put this to the test.

In the next bed space to mine was a Welshman called Ron Pugh. In civilian life he had been the manager of Wrexham Co-op. He told me of a devious plan he had been conjuring up for some time. Every second day a group of POWs had to collect the meat and vegetables for the entire camp. To do this they used four 2 wheeled carts which were normally pulled by pony or buffalo. The drill was one man between the shafts and two pushing from behind. The first three carts were loaded with vegetables, the fourth with meat. Given a choice the lads would avoid the meat cart as it was the heaviest but more importantly the vegetable carts always provided a chance to pinch an item or two off the cart and eat them in transit. On this occasion Ron Pugh, another POW and myself volunteered for the meat cart. On the return journey Ron produced a razor blade out of his hat and cut off a nice piece of beefsteak and then placed it back on the meat as if it was still intact. At the guard room the first three carts and their attendants were stopped and searched. We were waved straight through and as we proceeded through the camp Ron peeled off with his piece of meat whilst we delivered the meat to the central cookhouse. Ron had an Indian friend who cooked the meat for us and then delivered it in a tasty curry. Another example of how important food was to us. POWs regularly risked severe beatings if detected but were willing to take that risk in an attempt to supplement our meagre diet.

A job which we were required to complete on an outside working party tested our resolve to the limit. On three successive days we were taken to a place called Comyiran on the outskirts of Batavia. Here there was a deep drain which ran alongside the perimeter of what was once the civil airport. The drain was designed to catch any excess water in the monsoon season and then discharge it into an adjoining river. Over time it had become silted up resulting in it becoming a stagnant, dark green, foul smelling pool. We had to wade in bare-foot and scoop out the contents and place them on a bamboo raft. The water was thigh high and being bare-foot presented all sorts of dangers as you did not know what you were standing on. There were leeches in the water. They attached themselves to our legs and began their bloodsucking activity. Any attempt to knock them off only made them more tenacious and more painful. They were best removed by applying a lighted cigarette to their backs causing them to release their grip immediately. Inevitably the area of attachment became infected and ulcerous due to the foul water and poor state of health of the individual. History tells us that leeches once played an important part in treating certain conditions but I'm sure this would have been in a controlled environment unlike what we had just experienced. Our activity was a source of interest to the locals who gathered on top of the bridge. They must have found it rather amusing to see Europeans and some of their former Dutch masters now standing in stagnant water being bullied by the Japanese.

The 8 March 1944, the second anniversary of capture, came and went like any other day and shortly afterwards the Japs arrived in camp with boxes of

International Red Cross parcels. They then selected some of the healthier looking POWs and re-clothed them. A Japanese film unit arrived and filmed this but as soon as the unit had left everything was taken away. Blatant propaganda which would be distributed to show how well the Japs were looking after their prisoners.

Life in camp continued as normal but once again rumour struck. We were to be on the move again! The rumour was correct. We were to move on 14 May and were given two days to prepare. We were told that we could only take what would fit into one rucksack. That's all I had anyway. I learnt later that there were 1,937 men formed into two battalions. Predominantly British and Dutch but there were a few Australians. The average age of the British was 29 years and 36 years for the Dutch. Each battalion had its own Commander. Ours was Wing Commander P S Davis who would turn out to have a major influence on my later POW life. The Dutch Commander was W C Slabbekoorn. At this point it is appropriate to point out that the Japs issued an instruction that all officers above the rank of Major and Squadron Leader were to be housed in separate Officer Camps. Their rationale (as in their own Army) was that the separation would minimise the risk of revolt by the POWs as they believed that the ordinary soldier was incapable of thinking for himself. This was certainly the case so far as the Japs were concerned. Their soldiers hardly dare sneeze without the permission of a Senior Officer.

Now back to the move. The outgoing contingent included medical staff who, to everyone's astonishment, had been issued with medical equipment. This consisted of a microscope, an operating table and a limited number of medical instruments. A welcome move but hardly adequate given the number of personnel involved. We paraded in the dark at 6am and the usual Tenko took place. We were counted and re-counted as the Japs wouldn't accept the counting of our Officer in Charge. There was the usual confusion with shouting, jeering and the odd beating as the Japs became more and more frustrated. Eventually we moved off and marched to the nearest railway station at Pasir Senen. We boarded the waiting train and it moved off in the direction of Tanjong Priok the port of Batavia. There had been some speculation that this move would result in us going overseas. It looked like the 'speculators' were going to be right. The train took us right on to the quayside. We alighted from the train and, after another Tenko, the guards handed responsibility for us over to the ship's captain. His first instruction was to tell us to remove our mess tins from our possessions as we would not have access to our rucksacks once on board. At the top of the gangway we were instructed by a Jap soldier to go down into the forward cargo hold which meant climbing down a narrow wooden ladder. I saw that on the bridge front was a plaque showing that the ship had been built in Glasgow in 1923. The sailors amongst us worked out that the ship was 5000 British tons and didn't have enough life- saving gear for the numbers on board. We never did discover the ship's name but it was clear that its last load must have been coal as the hold was covered in coal dust. The hatch top was left open and the depth of the hold had been divided into two by a wooden platform built on wooden scaffolding. This effectively doubled the floor space but despite this there was still insufficient space for all the POWs. Our ruck-sacks were piled in the centre of the cargo hold and those POWs coming on board at the end of the Draft had to sleep on top of them or on the narrow footways around the stack. The cargo hold was severely over-crowded and it went without saying that in the event of the ship sinking their chances of survival was minimal. I'm sure each one of us was planning his escape route in the case of such an event. For those who suffered from claustrophobia it was disastrous. As they became more and more agitated they had to be restrained by col-leagues to prevent them from going up on deck as to do so would have resulted in a beating or even being thrown overboard. The Japs refused to accept that such a condition existed. Discipline on board was extremely strict. You were only allowed on deck to go for food or to the toilet. At 5pm the ship's engines started up and we moved out of the harbour. The two Commanders were told that the voyage would last for three days (two nights) but the destination and purpose was not divulged. We should reach our undisclosed destination at 5pm in the afternoon of the third day.

The air in the cargo hold soon became unbearable due to the heat and the smell of body sweat. The stench deteriorated and was made worse for those of us in the bottom part of the hold (below the wooden platform) as we had to suffer the consequences of those above suffer-ing from diarrhoea who couldn't make it up the ladder in time. Worse still was that we had no materials with which to clean up so it takes little imagination to realise that to sit in this environment for three days is degrad-ing to say the least. Thus the prevailing mood between POWs worsened hour by hour, resulting in quarrels and lpfffff+

the odd fight, which really achieved nothing! Those of us who had the strength to climb the ladder did get some exercise twice a day as we went for food. Meals consisted of rice and some watery soup. Water was rationed to two half cups per man per day. In the rear-most hold were 4,000 Romushas (slave labourers or Coolies). I will deal at length with the Romushas later. Going to the latrines also provided an opportunity for exercise. These were constructed from a wooden frame covered in gunny sacks. They stuck out from the side of the ship at deck height and were attached to the ships scuppers. The gunny sacks were meant to provide protection from the wind and rain but were totally ineffective. The total number of latrines was inadequate for the number on board which meant having to queue for some time. Waiting in the fresh sea breeze was most welcome unless you had to 'go' urgently and provided a welcome relief from the stench below. Whilst standing in the queue I noticed that we were being escorted by one small Corvette and from time to time a Jap combat plane circled overhead.

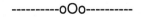

CHAPTER FIVE

Sumatra – building the Central Sumatra Railway Pekanbaru to Muaro – 137 miles

At the pre-arranged time of 5pm on 17 May 1944 the ship arrived at its destination of Emmahaven the port of the town of Padang on the west coast of Sumatra. Just before mooring there was complete silence which I later learnt is a Japanese tradition when a ship is about to dock. I have no explanation for this. The mooring hawsers were thrown out and then it all started to happen. The Jap guards and ship's crew barked out orders simultaneously, causing great confusion. What was clear was that they wanted us to disembark quickly. The Japs wanted everything done double quick. This wasn't happening as each POW was trying to find his rucksack from the pile causing quite a hold up. The Japs became very angry and kept shouting *'Hyaku, Hyaku'* (quickly, quickly) and then made the POWs disembark with or without rucksack. Those POWs who had been made to leave without their rucksack attempted to re-board. This annoyed the Japs as they couldn't understand why but they eventually got the message and commenced to throw the rucksacks down onto the quayside. This was disastrous for some as the height from which they were thrown easily damaged any fragile contents and worse still some never actually made the quayside but fell into the water meaning they were lost forever. Fortunately I was able to retrieve mine before disembarking.

We had to 'fall in' on the quay and were then told to sit down to await further orders. There was a lot of confusion. The Jap guards were noticeably agitated. Their Commander appeared confused. He gave orders and then countermanded them. We sat for all of two hours. Mercifully the sun was disappearing behind the horizon. It turned out that the Mayor of Padang had not been informed of the arrival of such a large draft of prisoners so accommodation for us had not been allocated. By now the POWs were also showing signs of unrest and this was being transmitted to the Jap guards. Rather interestingly, at this point, one of the more friendly guards confided that many of his colleagues were becoming concerned for their safety. Even though they were armed they were considerably outnumbered (there were 2,000 of us plus the 4,000 Romushas) so they felt quite threatened. No food or tea was provided but water was plentiful. At around 9pm we finally moved off in the direction of Padang. Progress was very slow as most of us were tired and hungry. The distance was about nine and a half miles. To make matters worse we then experienced a tropical thunderstorm. Everyone was soaked to the skin. Rucksacks became as heavy as lead. There were lots of stragglers who had to be helped. The Jap guards were already edgy due to the delay at the quay and the thunderstorm meant that they too were soaked. So the stragglers were just ignored so any belongings left along the road were lost forever. It was like being on a knife edge. Any minor event could have caused the guards to explode. A stab with a bayonet or even shooting was always a possibility. Best just to keep your head down. At about one o'clock in the morning we reached Padang. We were split into three groups. Group 1 went to the ex-Governor's residence. Group 2 to the Padang Civil prison and Group 3 (mine) to the local cinema. Another time for serious reflection. Even though I was tired, wet, cold and hungry I was still alive. Surely this was more than good fortune? Someone must be watching over me so it must be another case of 'Divine Intervention'. Let me explain. The conditions endured in the journey by sea were bad enough but, given that I was in the bottom section of the cargo hold, and being a non-swimmer, if the ship had sunk my chances of survival would have been almost nil.

At this point I would like to digress for a short while to relate the experiences of other POWs being transported in prison ships. For this I am grateful to a very good friend called Henk Neuman. A Dutchman, who formerly lived in the Dutch East Indies and latterly in Amsterdam. It turned out that Henk was in the Jaarmarkt with me and also on the same prison ship but we never met. It was only at a FEPOW re-union in Holland that I finally met up with him. Henk conducted in-depth research into the prison ships.

At 11.30am on 25 June 1944 a convoy of six ships left Belawan, a port on the north east coast of Sumatra, to sail down the Straits of Malacca bound for Singapore. One of these vessels was the 3040 ton MV Harikiku Maru, formerly the Dutch MV Van Waerwijk. On board were 724 POWs. At 2pm the following day the convoy came under torpedo attack. The Harikiku Maru and two other ships were hit and sunk. Despite the attempts of remaining vessels to save the casualties 178 POWs drowned. The attack took place just north of Tanjong Tiram and had been mounted by the British Navy submarine HMS Truculent commanded by Lieutenant R L Alexander. The Japanese vessel was not displaying the red cross in order to comply with International Rules of Sea so it appeared as any other merchant vessel and consequently was attacked.

The second, and by far the greatest shipping disaster in the Pacific War, took place at 4.15pm on 18 September 1944 off Bengkulu on the west coast of South Sumatra. The Japanese vessel MV Junyo Maru was torpedoed by the British submarine HMS Tradewind commanded by Lieutenant C Maydon RN DSO DSC.

The Junyo Maru was a freighter of 5015 tons owned by the Japanese Shipping Company Sanyo Sha Goshi Kaisha and at that time was operating as Japanese Military Transport No 652. On board were some 1500 POWs (predominantly Dutch but some British, Australian and US) and 4200 Romushas. The vessel had left Tanjung Priok and was en route to Padang where the prisoners and Romushas would be used to help build the railway from Pekanbaru to Muaro. She was being escorted by two small destroyers. After being hit the prison ship sank quickly, stern first. To avoid being hit themselves the two destroyers zig-zagged round the sinking vessel discharging depth charges at the same time. Once they felt that there was no risk of further attack the remaining vessels started rescue operations. The first vessel rescued the Japanese first and once up to its maximum (about 300 men) sailed immediately to

Emmahaven, arriving the following morning. The second vessel didn't commence to pick up survivors until after sunset and continued through the night. The following morning with approximately 300 survivors on board it sailed directly to the coast to discharge her passengers. Before leaving, the captain did shout that he would be returning. This he did but only after a long time. By the time he arrived it was dark and once he felt there were no more survivors he headed away to Emmahaven. Terrible scenes had taken place in those three fatal days. The Japs acted in a most brutal and inhumane way. Wounded and unconscious POWs were not rescued and some who had actually been picked up were thrown overboard again. When the second destroyer arrived at the coast it anchored offshore and was met by three Prahus (native vessels). These collected about half the number of survivors (their capacity) and took them as close to the shore as possible. From there the men had to wade through the water to reach dry land. They were barefoot and practically without clothing. Some were actually stark naked. The Prahus then returned to the destroyer to repeat the operation until all had been collected. Once on dry land they then had to follow a stream until they reached a road where they were put on lorries to travel the 145 miles to Padang. The 'tally' at the end of all this was 5620 POWs and Romushas perished and only 680 survived. This was war in its starkest form!

The survivors came under the command of a POW Naval Officer Lieutenant Commander Upton RNR who I had the pleasure of serving with much later. These survivors included those who had been taken directly to Padang by the first destroyer and those who had been beached and delivered by the Prahus. So I hope the reader acknowledges that to record the fate of these two prison ships is appropriate as it allows me to strike a comparison with my voyage, which, unpleasant as it was, did deliver me to another phase of my POW experience and, re-enforced my thoughts that, perhaps, someone up there was looking after me after all.

Now let's resume. We spent the night of 18 May in the cinema feeling the effects of tiredness, dampness, cold and hunger. Bread and tea was all that was provided. Next morning we were moved to the Civil Prison where we joined other POWs. What we found was most distressing even when considering what we had experienced so far. The whole area was soiled by the faeces of dysentery patients. The Jap command appeared content to simply ignore these conditions. The prison served as a transit camp for the Romushas. In a small room just inside the entrance were the bodies of twelve Romushas who had died the previous day. It transpired that death was a common occurrence particularly amongst the Romushas and it was the job of the POWs to take the dead bodies to the beach where they were cremated by the Japs. I have spoken earlier about the resourcefulness of POWs especially the British. Having a rank structure with authority certainly helps and facilitates the implementation of 'systems' designed to provide benefits for inmates. Straight away the POW command made the POWs dig holes to serve as latrines as the prison latrines were completely unserviceable. They then marked off the least soiled area of the camp to provide a 'rest' area. There was little or no disinfectant to help improve the situation and food was of the usual low standard. So things were quite desperate. Fortunately this wasn't to last as another rumour of a move began circulating. This time there was a rush of volunteers for the draft as a move would provide an escape from these dreadful conditions. I applied and was successful. On 19 May I joined the draft of 550 men and marched to the railway station at Pulau Air. This was the terminus of a branch line connecting to the central station in Padang. For some reason we were jeered at by the locals as we went along. As usual no-one knew our destination or the purpose of the draft. Some of the Dutch POWs were familiar with the area so were able to speculate as to possible destinations. They said that there weren't many alternatives as only one railway line served the west coast of Sumatra and went to a place called Padangpandjang. Here there was a junction where one line went to a coal mine at Sawahlunto and the other went to Pajakumbu. The latter was a single line which ran up a valley called Anei. After the valley the line climbed a steep mountain where it was so steep that a 'rack and tooth' centre line had been provided to prevent the train slipping backwards. The mountain was in the Barisan Range. Because it was single track there were many stops to check that it was clear to proceed meaning that the whole journey took one day. All this was described by a well-meaning Dutchman. As we approached Padangpandjang we wished the Dutchman had kept his mouth shut. Suspense was killing us. Will we be working in the coal mine or what will be our ultimate destination if we turn for Pajakumbu? Our thoughts also turned to the conditions at our next camp, surely they couldn't be any worse than Padang prison! We reached Padangpandjang and turned left. So we weren't going to the coal mine. We passed a town called Bukittinggi and eventually reached Pajakumbu. It was now quite late. No food or drink had been provided on the entire journey. The only drink we had was water from our personal water bottle, if you had one. We were accommodated in a school quite close to the station. It was a long building with a number of classrooms. It had a yard which was fenced with barbed wire. There were some latrines but insufficient for 500 men. There were two taps which served as washing facilities.

We quickly formed a cooking party but because there wasn't a kitchen we had to cook outside. The food ration was better than in the prison but was still insufficient. We slept on the concrete floor of the classrooms and next morning a fleet of Jap trucks arrived. These were partially loaded with provisions for the Japs and we boarded them with about 24 men to each truck. We hadn't a clue where we were going so at first we stood up but eventually sat down, which was wise, as we travelled all day! In the late afternoon we reached Pekanbaru. The distance from Padang to Pekanbaru is 228 miles (365km). We learnt that some later drafts had completed the whole journey by truck. On the train journey I recall crossing the Equator. It was marked by a large sphere of the world. On reflection I realised that this was the fourth time I had crossed it but this was the first time on land. When I crossed it for the first time on board the troop ship I was presented with a certificate from King Neptune. Unfortunately this was in kit bag No 2 which I abandoned long ago.

The trucks headed straight to our next camp which was to become known as Camp 1. On arrival we got another shock. On the site were some barracks made from bamboo and atap (palm leaves sewn to bamboo rods with rattan thongs). They were derelict and deserted. Some had roofs and walls missing and some had weeds and scrub growing inside. There were drainage ditches but these were overgrown and not fit for purpose. The whole place was a shambles. Not very welcoming for 500 tired, hungry, travel weary men. How long we were to remain here was uncertain. The Jap guards told us that we would be formed into working parties (not clear what we would be doing) and that we had four days to get the camp into some sort of order. Next morning we formed our own working parties and got to work bringing the camp into a habitable condition. Tools, equipment and materials to effect a proper repair were minimal so it was decided to concentrate on those barracks in reasonable condition and repair them by salvaging the material from those in the worst condition, some of which had collapsed completely. The Japs were never true to their word, nothing could be taken for granted so you lived in a state of complete flux. As was the case when the Jap Commander came and told us that we now had only had two days to complete the repairs as we were required urgently for the construction of 'A Railway'. This was the first intimation of what we were here for so let me expand a little on this topic. The Japanese Railway building unit was under the supervision of the 1st Battalion of the 9th Regiment of the Southern Army Rail Corps (SARC). In June 1942 they had been transferred from Burma to Central Sumatra to start preliminary ground works for the construction of a railway. The Japanese railway engineers had sound theoretical knowledge but seemed incapable of applying this knowledge in practical terms.

The result was that a lot of the work was sloppy, amateurish and quite primitive. The hard labour involved in creating the route was completed by the Romushas. This work involved cutting through dense jungle, creating embankments and cuttings in the most inhospitable environment. Work should have commenced in 1942 but the topographical difficulties had a considerable delaying effect. I will deal with this later.

So having mentioned the Romushas again, I think it is now time to provide a little more detail about them. At the time I had never heard the word. It was only later that I became aware of it and who they were. As stated earlier the word interprets as 'A forced labourer for the Japanese'. When the Japs first occupied the former Dutch East Indies they required large numbers of labourers to complete defensive works and other labour intensive work, sometimes in remote and sparsely populated areas. They organised several recruitment campaigns stressing to the natives that the work was for the defence of their own country and included incentives such as wages, lodgings, clothing and medical treatment. There were already food shortages on Java so the campaigns resulted in huge numbers volunteering. As soon as the first draft of volunteers had left, word got back to their families of the non-fulfilment of the Jap promises, the terrible working conditions and the high incidence of sickness and death. Consequently, the volunteers dried up so the Japs took an entirely different approach by just rounding up locals and forcing them to work for them. One method they used was to surround the local cinema and at the end of the performance arrest all the young men and take them to the railway station where they were placed in freight carriages and transported to Jakarta. Probably a day's journey without food and water. This was in March 1943 and from there they were transported by ship, roughly 4,000 at a time,first to Singapore and later to Pekanbaru on Sumatra. One of the ships transporting the Romushas was the Junyo Maru which was torpedoed and sunk off West Sumatra resulting in all the Romushas perishing (I mentioned this earlier). As the Japs became more desperate for labourers they even conscripted senior schoolboys, arresting them as they came out of school. On their arrival at Pekanbaru the Romushas were immediately subjected to a show of Japanese superiority. Eight were selected at random and required to lift up a length of rail. The rail was so heavy that they were unable to lift it. Their number was then reduced to six by the Japs and they were made to repeat the task. Obviously if eight couldn't lift it neither could six. They were then reduced to four and again made to repeat the task. The outcome was self-evident, but it didn't end there. These four were then beheaded with a samurai sword in front of the assembled Romushas. The Japanese Commander then informed the assembly 'A lazy Romusha can expect this'. From that point their grim life along the railway began. Insufficient food, no clothing, no wages and no medical treatment. They had to build their own shelter as they went along. These were generally temporary affairs made from bamboo and the leaves of the Nipa palm tree. Their diet consisted of one rice meal a day and if this wasn't available a tapioca porridge was provided. They would supplement this with vegetables or fruit scavenged from the jungle. They were working in mosquito infected areas but no nets were provided and medical treatment was out of the question. Most of them died from malaria, dysentery, malnutrition and tropical ulcers. They were particularly scared of the latter as these became so big that they prevented them from working. This effectively condemned them to death as the Jap motto was *'He who does not work shall not eat'*. At a place called Simpang Tiga was a so called hospital for them. The Romushas called it *'Rumah sakit simbolies'*. (symbolic hospital). If they were admitted they simply waited for death and if this took too long they were removed by the Japs and thrown into a mass grave on the other side of the road and buried alive. These mass graves could contain anything from 30 to 60 men. The Japs treated them worse than the POWs and quite often were heard to say *'Indonesia mati bagus'*(a dead Indonesian looks well) in the sense that only when he is dead is he a good one. As well as those buried in mass graves, any Romusha who died was buried on the spot, in the jungle, beside the road, beside the railway track, anywhere in fact. The graves were never marked. POWs frequently came across the bodies of dead Romushas lying in rivers or swamps and on occasions one would still be alive but on the point of death. POWs were strictly forbidden from helping a dying Romusha and would be severely beaten if caught ignoring this order. The total number of Romushas recruited by the Japs was estimated to be around 30,000. On the 15 August 1945 (when the Japanese capitulated) there were only 5,000 still alive. Even then their ordeal was not over as priority was given to the rescue of POWs rather than the Romushas and many waited to be rescued well after the war was over.

Romushas.
Reduced to skin and
bone. The death rate was
said to be around 80%.

As a footnote to this particular item I feel it is rele-
vant to point out that estimates of the number of
Romushas employed by the Japanese vary wildly. Some
estimates have been as high as 10 million but it is most
likely that this will include 'kinrohoshi' (unpaid labour-
ers) and some native auxiliary forces and arises because
the term Romusha was never strictly defined by the
Allies at the end of the war.

So let's now return to the building of the railway.
Many years beforehand the Dutch had surveyed a possible route for a Trans-Sumatra Railway but didn't
progress this as the route entailed the boring of some
sizeable tunnels. On the other hand the Japs cast this
obstacle and other topographical difficulties aside
believing that nothing could stop them. The Romushas
had already been deployed and had built the base earth
track. They had also created embankments and exca-
vated the small and medium cuttings. At the far end of
the track the larger cuttings had been left for the POWs

to prepare. Unfortunately, the Japs had not provided any special foundations where necessary and as large parts of the track had been built on soggy unstable ground some of the embankments slipped and some were actually washed away when it rained. This meant that bridges had to be built to allow the track to cross these areas. These were wooden bridges and were erected using a primitive pile driving method. They did stay in fairly firm shape if the embankments slipped but to the naked eye looked quite precarious. Additionally, the sides of some cuttings were too steep resulting in frequent landslides. All these failures had to be rectified by the POWs as they followed the route created by the Romushas. Obviously, this was very time consuming and seriously disrupted the Jap construction timetable.

The Japs formed us into gangs and gave each gang a name. These were 1Rope Men. 2 Marker Men. 3 Sleeper Men. 4 Rail Men. 5 Dassi Men. 6 Bar Men. 7 Hammer Men. 8 Noko Men and 9 Jointing Men. One thing that I would credit the Jap Engineers for was the track survey. Along the centre line of the proposed track there was a succession of short pegs. On the pegs were certain figures which indicated if the route was straight or curved and if the latter the radius of the curve was indicated. We were told by the Japs that to lose or break a tool or any of the equipment was a serious offence and would result in a beating. Once work commenced it was quite clear that they cared more for their tools than they did for the welfare of the POWs. On our first day out of camp we were taken to the rail terminal at Pekanbaru. Here we had to load rails and sleepers onto specially designed trucks. These were really two separate four wheeled trucks each with its own swivel base and brake column. The rails were loaded so that their ends rested on each of the trucks and when complete they were bolted down to effectively create one truck. Freshly cut and roughly hewn wooden sleepers were then loaded on top of the rails at each end of the truck. These were full of sap and very heavy. Once the loading was complete the POWs had to sit on the rails between both sets of sleepers to be taken to the work site. As the train moved along, the uneven track caused it to swing from side to side resulting in backsides being nipped or gashed by the rails. Having to concentrate on his personal safety often meant that the POW would lose whatever tool he was carrying with obvious repercussions as a 'tool tenko' was always carried out on arrival at the work place. Below is a sketch of the trucks I have described. A day's work would be to load and unload five or six of these trucks. The 'locomotive' used to pull the trucks was an old six cylinder diesel lorry which had been adapted for rail work. The front axle and wheels had been completely removed and replaced by a four wheeled swivelling bogey. The twin axle rear wheels had been removed and replaced by flanged brake drums of the correct width to fit the standard gauge rail. This would pull or push the laden trucks to and from the railhead. It was not very efficient as it often lacked traction and had difficulty climbing gradients without assistance from the POWs who had to jump off, push and then jump back on at the top of the gradient. To help overcome this as the driver approached a gradient he would put his foot down causing the trucks to sway violently resulting in backsides being 'wounded' as described earlier.

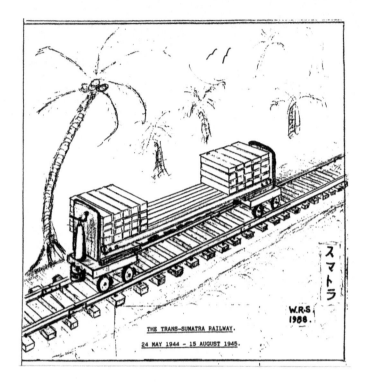

THE TRANS–SUMATRA RAILWAY.

24 MAY 1944 – 15 AUGUST 1945.

On this first day, at the railway depot, the Jap Engineer, a Sergeant, said *'Nippon-go hanashimasuka?'* (Does anyone speak Japanese?) Without hesitation and with little justification the rest of the gang pointed at me and said *'He does'*. This was most disconcerting. I did not speak Japanese. During my time in captivity I had built up and memorised a fairly extensive vocabulary of Japanese words which were intended only for my own use as and when required. As I mentioned earlier I thought it may allow me to eavesdrop on conversations between the Jap guards in the hope that I may learn something about the way the war was going.

I didn't realise it at the time but this event would, ultimately, have a significant impact on my future as a POW which will become apparent later. Each morning at the rail depot this Jap Sergeant would 'latch' on to me, particularly if things weren't going to plan, in the hope that I could prevent it getting out of hand. Unlike most of the Jap guards he was a quiet and friendly man who was easy to deal with.

Camp 1 was only some 200 yards distance from the River Siak. This flowed in an easterly direction. It twisted and turned, was narrow and deep in parts and wide and shallow in others eventually entering the sea at the Malacca Straits. It was navigable with care by day. The Japs had to import most of the material for the railway as resources locally were fairly limited. The rail lines were brought from Singapore up the River Siak where they were unloaded and stacked at the railway depot at Pekanbaru. Local labour provided the sleepers which were hewn from trees felled in nearby forests and jungle. Some of these were taken to the rail depot at Pekanbaru and as the line progressed they were taken to points along the line. Occasionally the POWs had to collect the sleepers from the jungle where they had been felled. In the monsoon season the jungle became a vast swamp where the water could be three feet deep in places. Ideally, the sleepers should be made from hardwood but these were generally sap-laden softwood of only reasonable quality. The Japs seemed to care little about quality as long as the quantity was there.

It is fair to say that none of us had any previous experience of building a railway. It was suggested that the system to be employed was a German one but I have no evidence to support this. There was no training, you were expected to simply pick it up as you went along although the role of each gang was explained briefly. I will elaborate. The Rope Men – These two men had a long thick rope which was marked at regular intervals with a highly coloured tape. They had to lay the rope so that it touched all the wooden pegs in the centre (mentioned earlier). Then came the Marker Man. He had a four foot pole with a short steel hook on the end. He simply scratched a line in the sand level with every one of the coloured tapes on the rope. This was to indicate the position of each sleeper. Then came the Sleeper Men. They worked in pairs carrying the sleepers from the rail truck to the points marked in the sand. Another man would then position the sleeper correctly on the track. The Rail Men probably had the hardest job. Each rail was carried on the shoulders of twelve men. Each rail was 15 metres long and weighed 570kg (1,266 lbs a little over 10cwt). Apart from its length and weight the footway at the side of the track was narrow and the soft soil made progress difficult. We were working right on the equator so the sun had heated the rail to the extent that shoulders and hands had to be protected with old rags to prevent burns and blisters. Then followed the Dassi Men. A dassi is an auger with a T shaped top used for boring a ¾ inch hole. Once the rail had been correctly positioned the dassi was used to manually bore a hole on both lower edges of the rail. Then came the Bar Men. Each man had a crowbar and a teak block. The rail was lifted by the crowbar and the teak block placed at the end of each sleeper. Whilst the Bar Man held the sleeper firmly the Hammer Man, equipped with a wooden shafted hammer with a 10 inch head, then hammered fixing spikes into the pre-drilled holes until their flanges gripped the bottom flanges of the rail. The Jointing Men then fitted jointing plates to the rails securing them with steel bolts which they tightened with ratchet spanners. I have deliberately left the Noko Men until now. The word Noko is an abbreviation of the word Nokogiri which is a large steel hacksaw. When laying a station or a passing loop, sets of points had to be fitted at each end of the by-pass length. This necessitated the sawing and drilling of the adjoining piece of rail. This was a laborious, slow and tiring task and, initially, it was not uncommon for the saw blade to break. There is a very simple explanation for this. The Japanese saw cuts on the 'back' stroke whilst the western version cuts on the 'forward' stroke so it was only after the operator became familiar with his Noko that the frequency of breakages reduced. Needless to say any breakage caused 'all hell' to break loose with the usual beating ensuing. Finally came the Gauge Man. The Gauge itself was a wonderful piece of kit and was almost sacred. It was made from polished and varnished hardwood and all the fittings were of highly polished brass. When not in use it was kept in a leather soft lined case. It resembled a large spirit level. It had two hinged pointers on the lower edge. One of these could be slid along and secured in any desired position. When the two pointers were at their nearest to each other this represented the standard gauge between the inside surface of the rail lines. 1.067 metres or 3'6". When the track bed was being prepared and a curve was required the Jap surveyors from the Railway Battalion would calculate a given radius and mark the centre pegs with an 'R' and a figure. When the Dassi man laid the rails the Gauge Man would reset the gauge to give an increased width between the rails. As the rails would only bend so far when cold it was difficult to 'gauge' accurately and sometimes (on purpose) the Gauge Man would be quite liberal with his settings. So it is little wonder that trains often became derailed and slipped down between the rails. Whilst this may appear counter-productive, as it created extra work for the POWs, it was quite satisfying for them to see the Japs becoming infuriated due to the lack of progress. After then end of the war the railway was inspected and the report, published in 1948, summarised it as 'Very inexpertly constructed'.

The railway would eventually cover a distance of some 137 miles and would be mainly single track. The first section was a four kilometre stretch from Pekanbaru to Tengkirang. Towards the end of this section the track took a sweeping right hand curve followed by a short straight where a level crossing was created to allow it to cross the main road at Tengkirang. Here Camp 2 was built and was to serve as the main camp for POWs for the whole of the rail project. The POW Commander at the Camp was Wing Commander PS Davis. On 28 May 1944 and only five days after starting work on the railway we moved to Camp 2. This was a much larger camp and in due course would serve as an administration and medical centre for all the other camps along the line. The Japanese Commander responsible for the POWs was a nasty man called Captain Myasaki. (After the war he was sentenced to death at a Court Martial held in Medan, North Sumatra).

Camp 2 was located alongside the Taluk-Tengkirang public road. A high bamboo fence had been constructed by the Japs to secure the camp from the outside world. It had quite good accommodation but as a kind of transit camp it had a shifting population. The healthier POWs went to other camps along the rail track whilst the sick ones remained for treatment and recuperation. It also served as a distribution centre of sorts for the other camps. POW drivers brought supplies (such as they were) from Bankinan on the road to Payakumbu for subsequent despatch to other camps. Because it was a medical centre it later held a great number of sick POWs so the death rate was extremely high. Sometimes there were as many as fifteen funerals a day. There were three cemeteries in the area but two of these became unserviceable as the water level became so high that bodies had to be pushed down with poles to allow the grave to be closed. The third and largest with 431 graves was on higher ground and across a small river (Sungei Tengkirang) that ran along the camp boundary.

Work on the railway continued as normal. This included the usual beatings when a Jap Guard would go berserk over some trivial matter. As the track progressed the daily journey to the work site got longer and longer. The British in true fashion and in an attempt to make life easier tried to instil some form of organisation in the Japs. For example, they tried to get the Japs to agree on the number of loads of rails and sleepers that would constitute a day's work. Let's say five. So we would say '*Go five trucks tomoray (finished) all men go home OK ka?*' Reply '*Hai OK*'. So next day the lads would work extremely hard and complete the five loads by early afternoon and go back to camp. However, next day the number of loads would be increased to six or seven. So much for the attempt to 'organise'. Ignoring the Japs, the sleeper men worked out a plan of their own. The number of sleepers expected to be delivered each day was counted and then divided by two (the number of men to each sleeper) providing the answer as to how many sleepers each pair must carry in a day. Sometimes this permitted one of the more frail POWs to be delegated as 'tally' man who simply counted the sleepers until the quota was met. It also allowed those who had completed their quota to rest at the side of the track away from the working area. Unfortunately the Japs didn't understand the scheme (or didn't want to) and would rouse the resting POWs insisting *'Hyaku, Hyaku takusan shin-goto'*.(Quickly, quickly, much work). A failure yet again! A reasonable Jap guard was a rarity indeed.

In early July I received a message that Wing Commander Davis wanted to see me. I duly presented myself. He was very accommodating and not at all intimidating. I will never forget the conversation. He said to me *'I understand you speak Japanese'*. I was stunned and said *'I've been helping when there has been trouble out on the railway line but I don't really speak Japanese'*. He then went on to explain that Camp 3 was about to be set up further up the line and that he wished to have an all British administration instead of the customary Dutch, and for that reason he required an English interpreter. I felt unnerved and thought his proposition was ridiculous. It was obvious that he was quite serious and concluded by saying *'I'll give you seven days to think it over'*. I left, a worried man. After seven days had elapsed I requested an interview with the Wing Commander and opened by saying *'I've thought it over and I'm not going'*.

He responded by saying *'I've thought it over and you are going'*. I lost sleep worrying over his decision. It came to pass and on 14 July I moved to Camp 3.

The camp was located at a place called Katabalu situated within a sweeping curve of the Kampar-Kanan River (Kanan meaning right). Further along there was a tributary called Kampar-Kiri (Kiri meaning left). It was in a low lying area and consisted of four barracks built from bamboo. Three of them faced end-on to a raised road leading to a Jap barracks. There was a separate building which served as a cookhouse. The Jap guard-room was on the other side of the road as was the Jap Commandant's house. The Jap CO was Lieutenant Nagai a young man with thick horn-rimmed specs which continually slipped down his nose. He had a pasty complexion suggesting that he may have been an admin man recently arrived from Japan. He did not admit to speaking English although I had a sneaking suspicion that he could. Our Commander was Captain Sydney Armstrong. We met for the first time. The camp doctor was Flight Lieutenant Braithwaite. The Adjutant was Lieutenant Dallas (a brave dashing young Hussar Officer) and his Hussar colleague Lieutenant Chadwick was the kitchen officer. The Acting Warrant Officer was CMS Hunt (the tattooed bully at Cimahi camp). I was recognised as the Official Camp Interpreter (who am I kidding) so wasn't required to go out on every working party. Still feeling quite unsettled over my new position I wondered when my first confrontation with the Japs might occur and how I might handle it. I didn't have long to wait. On the second day at Camp 3 one of our lads had to return to Camp 2 for some dental treatment. He travelled by Jap lorry. On the return journey he rode on the back of the lorry which was also carrying supplies for the Japs. Among the supplies was a bag of brown sugar. The temptation was too great. He helped himself to the contents and put them in his side pack. When he alighted from the lorry back at Camp 3 the Jap guard noticed traces of the sugar in the folds of his tunic. This resulted in him being searched when his 'booty' was discovered. All hell broke loose. If the lad didn't have toothache before he certainly did now, along with several other aches and pains from the severe beating he received. Lieutenant Nagai sent for me and instructed me to get the entire camp to parade in front of the barracks. This was when the fun began. Nagai was on my left. Lieutenant Dallas was on my right. Nagai spoke to me directly and, believe me, I didn't understand a word of what he was saying. When he paused, I turned to Dallas and said *'I don't know what he's going on about but I do know the subject'*. I then extemporized by saying to Dallas *'It is wrong to steal from the Imperial Japanese Army'*. Dallas repeated this to the assembled POWs. Judging by Nagai's reactions, it appeared to have the desired effect but he was still ranting on so I simply repeated what I had said earlier. At the back of my mind was the suspicion that Nagai understood English. It didn't matter, as he seemed to accept what was said and the parade was instructed to 'fall out'. However, this episode did have a sobering effect on me as from then on I made a determined effort to improve my Japanese. Shortly afterwards I received a gift of a Japanese-English text book and, although I will never know, I suspected that Wing Commander Davis had arranged this when he became aware of my predicament.

Food rations at Camp 3 were both inadequate and of poor quality. The supply truck would not venture down the muddy track from the camp to the road in case it got stuck. This meant that the supplies were dumped at the end of the track making them prone to theft by the locals. Getting them to camp proved difficult as all the fit POWs were out on working parties leaving only those SIQ in camp. The Jap guards wouldn't help taking the view that 'It's your food so it's your problem!' My problem was that I didn't have any authority to command a 'ration party' so I sought out someone who had. To this end I went to see CSM Hunt. He was most displeased as he didn't want to be seen as 'piggy in the middle' between the Jap guards and the POWs. He did arrange one 'ration party' but afterwards came to me and said '*The next time you need a ration party go and see somebody else*'. Now what do you make of that? Maybe it was a mistake on my part as despite all his rank I knew he was inwardly scared of the Japs.

The railway line ran close to the back of the camp and ended in the centre of the curve I mentioned earlier as it reached the Kampar-Kanan River. It was obvious that a bridge had to be constructed to allow the track to cross the river. A forbidding thought given the amateur-ish but forceful approach of the Jap Engineers. Materials for the bridge started to arrive. Most of the timber was sourced locally. Large numbers of long straight tree trunks were delivered. These were approximately 30 feet in length and 12 inches in diameter. They had been sharpened to a point at one end and the other end had been capped with a thick steel band, probably to prevent it splitting. Each one resembled a large pencil. On our side of the river the shore was sandy and slightly sloping. On the opposite side the bank rose steeply above the river. This had been created by the natural flow of the river in the huge curve. So building the bridge wasn't going to be easy. There was much speculation amongst the POWs as to how this was going to be achieved and the absence of any heavy machinery added to the speculation.

It soon became obvious and, yes, we were to be involved. On the sandy shore and quite close to the water a tall wooden tower was built. A heavy timber frame, similar in shape to goal posts, was attached to the tower and was placed so that it was leaning out over the river. A large steel pulley wheel was attached to the 'crossbar' section of the frame and a thick rope was threaded through the wheel.

The shore side end of the rope was spread out on the sand and had about 40 single ropes attached to it. A huge cast steel weight was attached to the river side end of the rope. This huge weight was then hoisted up to the 'crossbar' by, literally, hundreds of POWs pulling on the 40 or so ropes. The timber 'pencils' were manhandled into position in the river bed point first and held in position below the weight by POWs. The Jap Engineer then shouted '*Ici, Ni, No, Sanyo*' and at this point the POWs moved forward still holding the ropes allowing the weight to drop quickly on to the top of the 'pencil' creating a pile-driving effect. This continued until the 'pencil' had been driven into the river bed to the desired height. Four of these 'pencils' were grouped together about 12 feet apart and were stabilised by using diagonal timber supports. Groups of four 'pencils' were positioned in the river until the opposite side was reached. The groups of four were then 'tied' to each other. When completed the bridge looked slightly 'humped backed'. The reason for the 'hump back' became evident. When a train crossed the 'pencils' sunk into the river until the bridge was level but as soon as it had crossed they returned to their original position. On the upstream side of the bridge the POWs built breakwater piers in an attempt to control the flow of the river in the monsoon season.

In camp there were two deaths – Bombadier Sergeant Roy a British POW and a Dutch Infantry man called Meyer. They were buried at the foot of the railway embankment to the south of the camp and a 14 foot high wooden cross was erected. The Dutch Colonial soldiers, who were familiar with the ways of the East, said that once the ants got at it the cross would disappear.

The monsoon duly arrived and the river level rose quickly and dramatically. It overflowed its banks and soon the whole camp area was flooded to a depth of about 18 inches. Only the mud track remained clear as it was on higher ground. This really was a disaster. It meant that we were constantly walking around in stagnant water and even worse our beds were only some 3 to 4 inches above water level. Captain Armstrong asked me to go with him to see Nagai to ask if anything could be done. He wasn't interested. His attitude seemed to be *'I didn't make it rain'*. Subsequent requests met with the same result. Meanwhile, the bridge now had an acute down-stream 'bend' in it. POWs were sent to the piers to fend off any debris before it caused further damage and look outs were posted on top of the bridge to warn of the arrival of tree trunks or the like. The next day two huge winches arrived and were secured to each side of the river. Two wire ropes were then attached to the centre of the bridge on the upstream side. The POWs operated the winches until the bridge was pulled into its original position. The train was then sent over as if nothing had happened. As a matter of interest I learnt that a similar bridge crossing the Kampar Kiri River collapsed on 30 March 1945. Technically, the bridges were unsound because the groups of four 'pencils' were positioned too close together. Around mid- September (the camp was still flooded but the river level had receded) some more POWs arrived. They were survivors from the Junyo Maru sinking which I described earlier and were under the command of Lieutenant Commander HC Upton RNVR.

On 21 September 1944 there was another 'crisis' in camp. At Tenko one POW was missing. It proved to be a young Dutchman called Keyner. That evening Nagai sent for me. He was clearly annoyed. The escape had happened under his command and in typical Japanese fashion was scared of the consequences. He intimated that the matter would be handed over to the Kempetai (the Japanese Secret Police). They duly arrived that evening. I was called out, as was Nagai and two of his guards. We had to scramble up a slippery embankment at the rear of the flooded camp to reach the rail track. It was raining steadily. Here there was one of their diesel road-rail cars which we boarded. There were two Kempetai soldiers already on board. We were out all night on nothing more than a wild goose chase. Nagai and the guards were noticeably quiet in the presence of the Kempetai soldiers. I noticed that they were only 2nd Class Soldiers and the only way of distinguishing them from ordinary soldiers was a small brass cherry blossom badge behind their ordinary badge of rank. This badge had symbolic importance as it indicated that they had been chosen especially by 'Tenno-Heika' (the Emperor of Japan). Their authority was supreme so that, irrespective of their own rank, they could consider that all other officers and soldiers were answerable to them. They wielded this power with impunity, administering brutal punishment on the basis of suspicion only. No wonder Nagai and the guards treat them with suspicion throughout that wasted night. Thankfully POWs had very little contact with the Kempetai. On 1 October the escapee Keyner suddenly re-appeared at camp and gave himself up to the guards. He was sent to the Kempetai and after a severe thrashing was returned to Camp 3.

One of the Junyo Maru survivors was a chap called Jim (Ginger) Woods. He was in our unit at KL in the General Engineering section. He came from Gorleston on Sea, East Anglia. In civilian life he was a cinema projectionist. He had literally only the clothes he stood up in and a metal dixie. He told me that when I left the Jaarmarkt Camp to go to hospital he was one of the draft that had been sent to Haruku Ambon to build landing strips. He was then torpedoed by his own British Navy. How unlucky was that? On the other hand he had been extremely lucky to survive. We became good friends. Conditions in Camp 3 worsened as a direct result of the presence of the stagnant water which did not drain back into the river. Consequently the levels of sickness rose and the numbers available for working parties reduced. The only saving grace was that we saw little of the Japs as they rarely entered camp being frightened of catching even the common cold.

On 24 November Nagai sent for Captain Armstrong and myself to attend his quarters. In his hand he had the very first letters from home. He handed all but one of these letters to Captain Armstrong. He also told us that on 26 November we were to be moved to a new Camp 3 which was on higher ground. Also he told us that he would not be going. We thought that the escape episode had, perhaps, stalled his army career. He then instructed Captain Armstrong to leave but I had to stay. He talked to me about all kind of things and in particular about my family. I then realised that the one letter he had retained was for me. My father always used beautiful 'copper-plate' handwriting. I recognised it immediately. Nagai was cruelly teasing me by trying to read the letter out loud. Although he was sat on the other side of his desk I was able to read Dad's writing upside down quicker than he could read it the right way up. Finally he stuck out his hand to shake my hand and said 'Sayonara'. I had no desire to shake his hand but didn't have the nerve not to.

The move from Katabalu took us back along the railway line in the direction of Pekanbaru to a place called Kubang. A distance of just less than 2 miles. The conditions at the new camp were a welcome improvement after the flooding at the old camp. The Jap Commander at the new camp was Sergeant Major Tadaiti Ebinuma. He was older than previous Commanders and had an almost peasant look about him. Captain Armstrong and I went to his quarters to introduce ourselves and learn about the labour requirements of the railway engineers. We left with a very favourable impression, feeling that he was more accommodating than earlier Commanders. We also learned that all the guards at the new camp were Korean but were unsure how significant this might be. The only other Japanese was the Medical Orderly, a man called Osaki. There were 19 Korean guards and they had all been given Japanese names. Four of them were Guard Commanders, the rest rank and file.

All Far East Prison Camps were under the command of the 25th Japanese Army South East Asia with their HQ in Singapore. Initially the 25th Army was commanded by Lieutenant General Saito Yaheita who was later succeeded by Lieutenant General Tanabe Moritake. Both were sentenced to death by Court Martial at the end of the war as was the local Pekanbaru Commander Miyasaki Ryohei. Their crime 'rigidly carrying out inhumane orders. Prison guards were normally genuine Japanese soldiers but these were later supplemented by Koreans whose units were called Gunsoku. As it turned out the Koreans were more sadistic towards POWs than the Japanese. The explanation given for this is that when they were initially recruited they were given a promise that they would be employed in the economic rebuilding of the Japanese occupied territories for a period of two years. Instead they were appointed as wardens of the POWs. After two years their contracts expired so any agreements were null and void and they came under military control. Over and above this, Korea had been occupied by the Japanese for some time so the Japs adopted the stance of conqueror over defeated. So all members of the Gunsoku held a grudge against their Japanese masters. This manifested itself in their corruption, cunning and obstruction against the Japanese army who couldn't do anything about it as they needed the manpower. The Jap Commander of the POWs in the Pekanbaru area and along the railway line knew that POWs were being maltreated by the Korean guards but didn't do anything about it for fear of reprisals. Thus the Gunsoku soldiers felt untouchable and took this approach in their dealings with the POWs. So what were we in for here at the new Camp 3? In the course of my work as interpreter at Camp 3 I came into close contact with all of the Korean guards. Some encounters were friendly others quite distasteful. Later I will paint a brief 'pen-picture' of each one as I found him.

I was dismayed to learn that in the new camp there was a Dutch POW called De Jong who, before the war, had worked as a car salesman in Tokyo. He spoke fluent Japanese so my position as interpreter could be compromised as my command of the language was limited to say the least. I needn't have worried as De Jong was of such a nervous disposition that the Jap guards preferred me to him. There were times when we were both present and I learned a lot about the 'art' of interpreting from him. Most requests for my presence were to deal with 'hostile' situations between guard and POW. I quickly realised that applied psychology was a good approach in these situations. Once the Jap guard asked me to interpret his 'rant' I would then ask the POW for his response and finish by saying *'Just nod your head towards the Jap when I finish speaking'*. This worked on most occasions. The difficult cases were those that had occurred a while before my arrival. I had to quickly 'grasp' the issue and try and deal with it. In a lot of cases it was quite clear that the POW had broken the rules so I simply tried to mitigate the outcome, particularly the punishment, not always successfully. I was fully aware of the importance of my role and would always try to defend the position of the POW. Sometimes this was impossible, particularly if it was a serious breach of the rules. I recall many occasions when I took a 'creative' approach by not interpreting the Japs words correctly in the hope that corporal punishment might just be avoided. This didn't always work as there were those occasions when the Jap was determined to inflict severe punishment irrespective of what was said. Other difficult situations to deal with were those when I had no choice but to tell the POW that his chances of getting off were limited. There were even cases where the POW would accuse me of wrongly stating his case and I recall once being accused of 'siding with the enemy'. Heaven forbid! Finally, the Jap guard's temperament was often quite unpredictable and difficult to 'read'. They could be calm one second and 'explode' the next. So, whilst the role of interpreter may have been seen by some POWs as a cushy number, let me say quite clearly that it wasn't. I had to try and keep both 'parties' happy to ensure the smooth running of the camp which wasn't easy but was always my overriding consideration.

Every evening Captain Armstrong and I had to meet with Ebinuma to discuss the requirements for working parties for the next day. A form called a 'Nippo' had been introduced by the Japs. The POW Office staff in conjunction with the MO had to declare on the form the numbers of 'fit' men available for work, the number in sick quarters and the number in hospital. If done correctly this would account for all POWs. So the completed 'Nippo' was handed to Ebinuma who already possessed the requirements of the railway engineers for the next day. On many occasions the 'demand' was greater than the 'supply'. Ebinuma would shake his head and say '*Mushkassi-na*' (difficult) and so it was. In his defence he quite often negotiated with the engineers when their numbers couldn't be met and reached a compromise where the sick were allowed to remain SIQ.

Because we had moved to new camps so frequently, the British in particular, were very good at getting organised. Fatigue duties were allocated and top of the list was always the preparation of proper latrines. Their location was important. Not too far away from the barracks and not too close as they soon began to smell. The position of the cookhouse was also important and a quiet corner for the sick bay was selected if at all possible. A small section of Barrack No 2 was set aside as an office as we had to complete forms for the Japs but they never seemed to ask for them except, perhaps, the 'Nippo'. They even provided a typewriter which I think Noah had abandoned.

Rations, both the quality and the quantity, were important to all POWs. Sufficient to sustain those expected to undertake physical work outside and also to aid the recovery of those SIQ. But we never seemed to receive the required amount. I later learnt that the level of daily rations had been officially laid down. This is shown below together with a comparison of what was actually provided.

	Official	Actual
Rice	400gms	300gms
Vegetables	300gms	100gms
Tapioca flour	60gms	100gms
Salt fish/meat	30gms	30gms
Oil	20gms	20gms

As a result of the vegetable shortage special parties (under guard) would forage in nearby woods or jungle for wild fruit and vegetables such as Passi-Flora (passion flower), ginger root and the tops of various edible ferns. Occasionally, a rambutan would be found. Meat was always in short supply and even when it was provided it consisted mainly of cow head without tongue, bones and intestines. As meat was seen as essential part of the western diet POWs became quite proficient at catching snakes, rats, monkeys, racoons and dogs and consuming them. After a while in captivity at Camp 3 Captain Armstrong and I got permission from Ebinuma to buy a water buffalo from a local farmer. I will describe this later. This was a feast after a famine. We used everything except the hooves, horns and eyes. Its gall was used by the MO. Its hide was dried in the sun then sliced and fried. The bones were burnt until white and brittle then ground down into a white powder which was given to the sick as a calcium booster. In one corner of the camp we created a 'Dedek' factory. Here we boiled rice husk over and over again until it formed a type of liquor. This was said to be rich in vitamins and was injected into all POWs by intra-muscular injection. As in previous camps we were instructed by the Japs to create a vegetable patch. This necessitated clearing an area of scrub which was located just to the side and rear of the Jap Guardroom. Now all good gardens need some form of fertiliser and the obvious source for this was the latrines. Necessity is the mother of invention so we made some 'waterproof' square boxes which were fitted with rattan handles. These were lowered into position in the bottom of the latrines and when full were carried on a bamboo pole by two POWs to the vegetable patch. Obviously, the smell was quite offensive but the two POWs became so accustomed to it that they hardly noticed it. To reach the patch the two POWs had to exit the main gate in front of the guardroom. Orders meant that anyone entering or exiting had to present themselves to the guard, bow and continue. The two POWs would deliberately stop, place the box on the ground, bow very slowly and then continue slowly to the patch. The Jap guards soon got fed up of this and created a hole in the fence to allow them to reach the patch without having to pass the guardroom.

During the scrub clearing process lots of insect life was disturbed. We had no protection and, unfortunately, Captain Armstrong was bitten. As a result he contracted typhus (as opposed to typhoid) and became seriously ill. He lapsed into unconsciousness and was hospitalised. Since arriving at Camp 3 Captain Armstrong had built up a good rapport with the Korean guards. They looked on him as a sort of 'father' figure. His rationale was that it allowed him to diffuse difficult situations. It worked as the guards rarely got angry with him. The Dutch didn't like it as they saw it as fraternising with the enemy. One day a guard called Kanimitsu (he had a mouthful of gold teeth) approached me and said 'Shoko doko Deska?' (Where is the Captain?) I replied 'Shoko byoki desu'. (the Captain is ill). Kanimitsu looked genuinely concerned and said 'Takusan byoki Deska?' (Is he very ill?) I replied 'Hai, takusan byoki Desu'. (Yes, he is very ill). He then asked if the MO had any medicine for the Captain. I said 'No' The following day he called me over and gave me a supply of M and B tablets and said 'For the Shoko'. I gave the tablets to Doc Braithwaite feeling that it wasn't my position to give the tablets straight to Captain Armstrong as there may be more deserving cases in camp. Doc reasoned that as the tablets were obtained specially for the Captain, otherwise they wouldn't have been provided, they should be given to him. They assisted in his recovery.

The incidence of dysentery rose rapidly. The latrines were crude to say the least. Toilet paper had passed into oblivion. It's worth pointing out that the natives never used such things, preferring to use a bottle or gourd filled with water and wash themselves manually. In pre-war days they would boast that they were 'cleaner' than westerners. The latrines had been constructed over a deep pit with closely fitted wooden planks to create the floor. Ten removable lids were provided where 'business' was to take place. At one end of the latrines a purposely smoky fire was lit with a chimney at the other end to draw the smoke through. This was to try to kill the maggots down below. But the smoke could make it difficult to position oneself accurately and it was not unusual to see 8 or 10 men squatted there crying their eyes out!

Work on the railway line continued. Just outside the camp a siding had been created off the main line. This terminated just below a sandy cliff. Large rail trucks were placed on the line in the siding and these had to be loaded with sand from the cliff. As usual the method was quite primitive and involved manual labour. Each POW was provided with a 'chunkel'. This is a type of pick cum spade where the spade portion is fixed at right angles to the shaft. The spade portion was used to load sand into shallow baskets which were then carried by POWs on their heads and tipped into the trucks. Once three trucks were full they had to be pushed manually onto the main line and then into the nearby jungle where the sand was used to re-build the washed away embankments. This part of the work was supervised by the railway engineers whilst the loading of the trucks was supervised by the guards. One particular day there was one solitary Jap guard supervising the loading. He was small, very young and looked as if he was a 'rookie' recently arrived from Japan. It was another of those occasions when the guard was trying to 'wind up' the POWs. He kept shouting *'Iggerisu Damay denah'*. (Englishmen are useless). One of the POWs was a chap called Bernard Bastin from Reading. He was nicknamed 'Cliff' after the legendary Arsenal footballer. I don't think anyone knew his proper name. The Jap continued to chunter at the POWs. The intense heat and the continual moaning eventually got to Cliff and he 'snapped'. He raised his chunkel towards the Jap and pinned him against the cliff face. He turned pale, looked extremely frightened and instead of administering the customary beating simply walked away. No-one was more surprised than Cliff. That night Captain Armstrong and I made our usual visit to Ebinuma to deal with the next day's work. Ebinuma came straight to the point. The attack had been reported by the railway engineers. The man had to be found. To this end, the next day, I was to go out with the working party and one of the Korean guards to try and identify the man. I already knew that it was Cliff so I got a message to him telling him to keep his head down. The Korean guard turned out to be a man called Kobayashi (alias King Kong). He was a large pigeon-toed nasty individual. He and I set about looking for Cliff. It was apparent from his demeanour that Kobayashi was determined to find him so that he could give him a beating. At one point we sat on top of the loco to get a better view of the working party and all day long Kobayashi kept asking if I had identified him. I never did understand why the Jap guard wasn't used to help identify him. The day passed without an identification so it was either a success or a failure depending on your standpoint! Back in camp Captain Armstrong, who was now on the mend, was relieved to hear that nothing had happened. But he decided that when Cliff returned to camp the three of us would go and see Ebinuma and admit the offence. This was sound thinking as it would allow us to 'lose face' which was important in Japanese military culture and might obviate future reprisals. As the three of us were waiting to enter Ebinuma's office who should pass by but Kobayashi. He was on his way for a bath and said to me '*Is that him?* I said '*Yes*'. His disappointment was quite apparent. He had missed his opportunity to give Cliff a beating. Afterwards I advised Cliff to avoid Kobayashi at all costs.

I referred earlier to the Gunsoku contingent of Korean guards at Camp 3. Here is the list along with the nicknames (in brackets) they came to be known by-

KANAYAMA	Guard Commander and Rations Official
ABBE	Guard Commander (The Yid)
HIROWKA	Guard Commander (The Dead End Kid)
MIYAMA	Guard Commander (Neurotic)
HARADA	Soldier – wore thick specs. Not to be trusted.
INUEE	Soldier (The Basher)
ISHIMOTO	Soldier (Rubber Neck)
KANASHIRO	Soldier (The Wrestler)

KANIDA	Soldier Little known about this one.
KANIKURA	Soldier (The Old Man) Not too bad.
KUNIMOTO	Soldier (The Bagoose Heitai' = The good soldier)

He gave himself this name

MARUYAMA	Soldier (The Shy One) He spoke a little English.
MITSUI	Soldier (Gladys) Effeminate.
NARAIYA	Soldier He was friendly with Mitsui!
NIHIDA	Soldier (The tall one) Unusual for a Korean.
SOEKAN	Soldier (The Pig. Dutch 'Varkenskop')
YANAGAHARA	Soldier (The Aga Khan)
KANIMITSU	Soldier (The Chinaman) Had a moustache and gold teeth.
KOBAYASHI	Soldier (King Kong)

After the war most of the Guards appeared before war tribunals charged with cruelty or neglect of the POWs in their charge. So far as the above guards are concerned records indicate the following-

KANAYAMA – death by hanging. MIYAMA – acquitted. KANASHIRO – 12 yrs imprisonment
KANIDA – 5 yrs imprisonment. KUNIMOTO – 15 yrs imprisonment. MITSUI – 8 yrs imprisonment
YANAGAHARA – 14 yrs imprisonment. KOBAYASHI – death by hanging. It appears that KANAYAMA

received the death penalty as he was the rations officer and was accused of deliberately withholding them. KOBAYASHI received the death penalty to reflect his extreme brutality towards POWs.

Security at the camp was minimal as the perimeter was marked by only two strands of barbed wire. The usual custom was for the Guard Commander and his shift to sit in the guardroom. Sometimes for hours on end. Occasionally they would make a single circuit of the camp just inside the perimeter fence. Escape would have been easy but futile as the colour of your skin would have given you away immediately. Additionally, the Japs had promoted the South East Asian Co-Prosperity Sphere which, basically, translated as 'Asia for the Asians'. This meant that natives would delight in reporting escapees for small reward. I mentioned earlier the unpredictable nature of the guards. This meant that POWs tended to keep them at arms-length. There were occasions when it was possible to have a reasonable conversation with them and others where they would 'blow up' over some trivial matter. My role as interpreter brought me into regular contact with them and allowed me to build up a profile of each one, noting his good points (if he had one) and his likes and dislikes. One day Kobayashi (incidentally Koba means tiger and Yashi mean jungle so he lived up to his name) sent for me. He asked me if the camp kitchen could use a bulk supply of dried red beans. A silly question. Obviously they could. So I told him. He said '*Choto matay*'. (Wait until I see you again). Next day he told me what price they would be and that he had bought two large sackfuls which would be delivered shortly. On no account should Ebinuma get to know of this. To our surprise the Jap Railway Engineers had introduced steam locos on to the railway. These passed close to the camp in each direction at least once a day. Kobayashi had arranged for the evening westbound train to drop off the sacks as it passed the camp and the driver would confirm the 'drop' by hooting twice. My role was to arrange for four men to collect the sacks and deliver them to the kitchen. There was no guarantee what time the train would be arriving and as it was getting dusk I wanted to go to bathe before the mosquitoes arrived to attack me. So I arranged for my Dutch Interpreter friend De Jong to look after Kobayashi's plan and listen out for the train and the two hoots. I took my time bathing and then returned slowly to the camp. As I approached the railway line, to my annoyance, I saw the two sacks lying beside the line just where they had been dropped. I rushed back to camp and found De Jong. He had forgotten. Kobayashi hadn't and he came at me like a raging bull. Obviously he didn't want his corrupt activities to become common knowledge or known by Ebinuma. I managed to placate him and arranged for the sacks to be recovered. Whilst the POWs were benefitting from his deceit he was also making a huge profit at their expense. Kobayashi wasn't alone. This sort of corrupt trading by the guards was rife. Even worse Ishimoto and Kanida actually pinched items from the official rations and then sold them to the POWs for whom they were originally intended. Conversely, the POWs themselves were very resourceful when it came to supplementing what little income they received. Cloth and textiles were in great demand by the natives and would bring a good price when sold. The POWs placed this enterprise in the hands of two trustworthy lads; Dave Spero, a London Jew and Paddy Davin, an Irishman (obviously). Most POWs kept a shirt and pair of shorts for 'better days' but from day to day the wearing of a Jap style 'Fundoshi' (known affectionately in camp as 'G' strings) became almost universal. This was made from a piece of cloth 2'6" long and 8" wide. One end had a length of tape attached to it. To wear one, the cloth was allowed to hang behind the body and the two ends of the tape were brought around to the front of the body and tied in a bow. The hanging cloth was then brought through the legs to the front and tucked through the tape. This meant that certain items of clothing, such as underpants, were now redundant and could be sold for profit to the natives. Dave and Paddy's daily task was to go into the jungle to fell trees and carry them back to the camp kitchen to be used as fuel. Clandestine meetings had been arranged with the natives who would squat in the jungle out of sight of the Jap guards and armed with Japanese paper money purchase the daily offerings. The income was a shared resource being paid into the camp exchequer.

It soon became known that Camp 3 was the best organised of all the camps along the railway line. This was the first and only camp to be administered solely by the British so we felt a sense of great pride in achieving this unofficial accolade. So I think it is entirely appropriate to place on record the constituent members of the admin staff –

Captain S Armstrong RASC - Camp Commandant
2nd Lieutenant RJG
   Dallas Hussars   - Adjutant

Flight Lieutenant RF Braithwaite RAF	- Senior Medical Orderly
2nd Lieutenant Chadwick RAF	- Kitchen Officer
Father Patrick Rorke SJ	- Padre
AC WR Smith RAF	- Interpreter
Bombardier Nichols RA	- Chief Clerk
Private G Hull RAMC	- Medical Orderly
LAC J Macauley RAF	- Medical orderly
CPO Thomas RN	- Quartermaster

Whilst I cannot recall their names it would be remiss of me not to mention our two cooks. They were both Royal Artillery men and had the unenviable task of having to prepare meals from the meagre rations supplied by the Japs. Regularly they performed miracles, especially on festive days, when they never failed to provide some sort of festive meal. To their additional credit, they sat down with pen and paper, designed and then built a fully functioning mud oven. They used this to provide a type of bread bun from ground tapioca root. Not entirely 'hovis' but very acceptable and a welcome change from our normal diet.

Doc Braithwaite and the two MOs also performed miracles. Medical equipment was limited and the only medicines they possessed were those that they were able to retain from pre-captivity days as the Japs didn't supply any. The sick bay was primitive. Equipment had to be sterilised in the cookhouse and operations were performed in barely hygienic conditions. The jungles of Sumatra were breeding grounds for malaria carrying mosquitoes and it was well known that this part of the world was one of the highest producers of quinine used to combat the disease. After the Jap invasion production of this medicine came to a halt so it was in short supply. It is derived from the bark of the Cinchona tree. The Japs did provide some plain ground cinchona bark but its quinine content was very low, probably no more than 10%. This powder was given to POWs suffering from Malaria (most of them). It tasted horrible and caused dizziness. Old wet rags were used as bandages and latex from the local rubber trees served as sticking plasters. The poor state of health of the POWs, together with the poor diet, meant that the simplest skin abrasion could quickly erupt into a running tropical ulcer. The general treatment was to wipe away any excess pus and then attach maggots to the infected area. These would eat the dead tissue around the ulcer in the hope that this would encourage the growth of new skin around the infected area. The camp did have a Jap Doctor, Lieutenant Ishi, but he was useless as he was obviously under instructions from his Command not to provide anything which might improve the lives of POWs. So the reader might reasonably presume that these dire conditions would have a detrimental effect on the mental state of the POWs. I can state with some pride that in all my time in captivity I recall only two instances of depression and mental instability which, I believe, speaks volumes about the steadfastness of the POWs.

During this period there were four POWs who were very ill. They were to be transferred by train to Camp 2. Captain Armstrong wanted a confidential letter taking to Wing Commander Davis at Camp 2 so for one day I was to act as a travelling MO. I was issued with a Red Cross 'Wan-sho' (armband) and went with these very sick lads on the train. All four were suffering from the advanced effects of Beri-Beri. This occurs when the body is starved of Vitamin C and other vital nutrients. It manifests itself by localised water filled swellings. In one example the face can become so swollen that the individual becomes unrecognisable. In another example it might attack the ankles and lower legs. These would swell and give the appearance of elephant's feet. In males it could affect the genitals. These four lads were affected in this way. Without exaggeration their testicles had swollen to the size of footballs making it impossible for them to wear any clothing on their lower body. They had to carry their testicles to relieve the pain from them hanging down. Within four days they all died – just another statistic!

I met with Wing Commander Davis who presented me with a pair of pig-skin Jap boots (I don't know why) and also gave me a confidential letter to take back to Captain Armstrong. I never did discover the contents of the two letters.

Whilst in Camp 3 Captain Armstrong and I would seek permission from Ebinuma to hold concerts. These requests were almost always granted. When making these requests I would be required to speak to Ebinuma in Japanese and whilst doing so Captain Armstrong would, by both action and sound, imitate a trombone. This was most annoying and quite unnecessary. It didn't appear to unsettle Ebinuma. He probably thought the Captain was just another of those eccentric English gentlemen. The concerts were always colourful, entertaining affairs. We had a rich source of untapped talent meaning they were produced to an almost professional standard. They were generally presented and directed by Albert (Steve) Stephenson, who, after the war, became a prominent Radio and TV producer. The concerts were enjoyed by everyone. They had an uplifting effect and a positive impact on camp morale.

Shortly after one of the concerts I was called to the guardroom by Kanashiro (The Wrestler). I noticed straight away that he had lost weight. It was most noticeable in his face. I remember most clearly that he forgot himself and spoke to me in Korean. He said '*Igo beyer*' which translates as 'I have severe stomach pain'. He asked if I could arrange for him to be seen by one of the camp MOs. I knew that Doc Braithwaite disliked him so I took him to see one of the Dutch MOs and set about translating both ways. The MO examined Kanashiro's lower abdomen and then in Dutch said to me '*Ik zullen nooit ons medicijn geven naar deze idioot. Ik zullen inboorling medicijn aanraden*' which translates as 'I shall never give our medicine to this idiot. I will advise local medicine'. He then advised that Kanashiro should not eat, take only liquid such as coffee and then consume 'Roti bibit merah', the seeds of a kind of red pumpkin which are normally thrown away. Then when 'nature calls' he must preserve the results for examination by the doctor. When this happened Kanashiro called the doctor and me to the back of the guardroom and pointed to his 'results'. The doctor then prodded and poked them which (to my complete surprise) revealed a 10' long tape worm. To satisfy his professional curiosity the doctor searched for the tape worms head and was happy once he found it. Kanashiro returned to good health. Not a nice story but interesting nevertheless.

PLAN OF CAMP 3A - KUBANG, SUMATRA

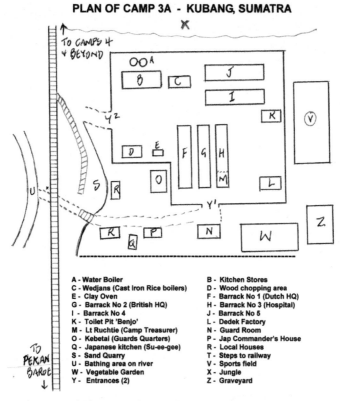

A - Water Boiler
B - Kitchen Stores
C - Wedjans (Cast Iron Rice boilers)
D - Wood chopping area
E - Clay Oven
F - Barrack No 1 (Dutch HQ)
G - Barrack No 2 (British HQ)
H - Barrack No 3 (Hospital)
I - Barrack No 4
J - Barrack No 5
K - Toilet Pit 'Benjo'
L - Dedek Factory
M - Lt Ruchtie (Camp Treasurer)
N - Guard Room
O - Kebetai (Guards Quarters)
P - Jap Commander's House
Q - Japanese kitchen (Su-ee-gee)
R - Local Houses
S - Sand Quarry
T - Steps to railway
U - Bathing area on river
V - Sports field
W - Vegetable Garden
X - Jungle
Y - Entrances (2)
Z - Graveyard

Former Camp 3 occupied from 14.7.1944 to 26.11.44 when it closed due to flooding. Camp 3A occupied from 26.11.44 to September 1945.

Above is a plan of Camp 3A at Kubang which, I hope, will allow the reader to identify those areas I have mentioned in this narrative.

For example 'W' is the veg patch.

'S is where Cliff Bastin had the run in with the little Jap. 'Y²' is the

entrance/exit used by Dave Spero and Paddy Gavin to access the jungle 'X'. 'U' is where the beans were dropped. 'P' is Ebinuma's house and 'O' is the Kebetai.

You will remember Jim (Ginger) Woods the survivor of the Junyo Maru sinking. As I mentioned earlier, he had only the clothes he stood up in. I was lucky as I had a 'Klambu' (mosquito net) which was absolutely essential after dark. We agreed to form a two man 'Kongsie' where we shared the Klambu. I got him a job as 'Kebetai Toban' which sounds quite interesting but is simply Korean Barracks servant. It entailed keeping the barracks clean and doing the laundry down at the river but it excused him from railway working parties. A European as servant to Koreans! Who would have believed it?

Christmas 1944 came and went almost unnoticed. We did have a day off and the cooks tried to prepare something special for lunch. We held a carol service which raises an interesting point. The Japs never interfered in anything of a religious nature so such meetings could be held freely. The odd Jap guard might look in but only to satisfy his curiosity. Kobayashi and Maruyama claimed to be Christians but never provided any evidence in support. We had a Padre in camp but if he was missing for any reason it was not unusual for a layman to take the Service. This happened on many occasions. Bibles were becoming scarce. Most had gone up in smoke as the pages were used as cigarette papers. Even small denomination Japanese banknotes were used as cigarette paper. Most of life's necessities were in short supply as Red Cross parcels were strictly controlled by the Japanese. After the war I was frequently asked by former European POWs or their relatives '*How many Red Cross parcels did you get?*' It would not have been untrue to say '*None*' as we had only one delivery in all the time in captivity. I remember it well. Each parcel was marked 'For 4 persons' but the Japs had helped themselves to anything that took their fancy and what was left was distributed one parcel to 40 persons. Interestingly, after the Japs capitulated a Jap storeroom at Pekanbaru was found to be full of Red Cross parcels along with some one year old mail intended for POWs and other internees.

New Years Day 1945 was our third in captivity. To recognise this special occasion the lads produced a raucous rendition of Auld Lang Syne. This resulted in me having an interesting and rather heated argument with Miyama who was the Guard commander that day. He said to me *'That Japanese song'*. I didn't agree and told him so. He went on to say that it was a Japanese College song which was sung on graduation day. I said to him *'That Scotterando song so there'*. Nothing came of the argument but it was always dangerous to get into conflict with the Gunsoku for the reasons I have mentioned previously. On the other hand Maruyama (the shy one who spoke some English) quite often sat in our barracks and conversed with me. I understood him well. He was trying to be 'matey' for his own benefit. On one occasion he explained a Japanese tradition relating to babies. He told me that no matter when a Japanese baby is conceived, on the day of its birth it is 1 year old. So all the Japanese have their birthday on New Years Day. It is called 'Tan-yobi'. I suggested to Maruyama that this was daft. He asked why? I explained that a baby born on New Years Eve would be two years old the next day. He didn't seem to understand.

In mid-February 1945 I witnessed an event that will never escape my memory. It was the worst occurrence in all my time in captivity. I apologise for the length I have taken to explain it but feel that this is necessary to do it justice. It happened on what would have been another normal day in camp. Every second week some of the Gunsoku (by rota) were given a half day's leave on a Wednesday afternoon. Those on leave would change into their best uniform and walk up the railway line to a small village called Simpang Tiga. Here there was a building which had been set aside for the sole use of off duty soldiers. In the building there were Geisha Girls and part of it was used as a brothel. Please remember, Geisha Girls are not prostitutes, they are there to entertain the males by singing, playing musical instruments and serving tea and the Japanese national drink sake (rice wine). It was not unusual for the Gunsoku to get drunk and return to their Kebetai in a drunken state. Nothing wrong with that! On this occasion Inuee (The Basher) appeared through the main gate dressed only in his Fundoshi. He was clearly drunk and was waving a bayonet in the air. The guards on duty did nothing at all and appeared quite amused by his behaviour. I witnessed this from the doorway of Barrack No 2. Suddenly Inuee called out in Japanese *'Smissu, minna-minna shoko nara bei'*. (Smith, get all the officers out on parade.) I had no option. All the officers paraded, albeit reluctantly. In front of the assembled officers Inuee then let out a tirade which was difficult to understand but can be translated roughly as *'Officers and prisoners are conquered beings, in fact slaves of the lowest order and but for the goodness of the Koreans would all have been dead long ago'*. His drunken state caused him to lapse into speaking Korean which rendered my services useless. He was unsteady on his feet and making reckless strokes with the bayonet. He kept asking those officers present the same question '*Are Koreans good soldiers?*' Whether he expected a reply was not certain but in any case, given the circumstances, it would have been remiss to say 'No'. The single line of officers with the Dutch on the left and the British on the right stood there defenceless. In the British section was a bearded Merchant Navy man (in other words a civilian) who really should not have been a prisoner. Suddenly, Inuee went berserk and slashed one of the Dutch Officers on the left jaw with the bayonet. I remember a slight delay but blood began to pour out on to the Officer's shirt. This seemed to give Inuee fresh impulse as in the next second he struck the Merchant Navy man on his chest with the bayonet inflicting a deep wound. As if this wasn't enough he then struck him on the head. To this day I recall my thoughts at this time. I was saying to myself 'This is a dream. It can't be happening'. Inuee then approached Captain Armstrong and they fixed each other with an unflickering stare. He never touched Captain Armstrong. He then moved along the line and confronted the Dutch Commander Captain Soeters cutting into his left shoulder with the bayonet and again drawing blood. In the line was Lieutenant Commander Upton (ex Junyo Maru) who had been roused from his malaria sick bed to attend the parade. He looked dreadful but this didn't preclude him from being attacked. Inuee hit him on the head. The next for 'treatment' was a Dutch Warrant Officer who was also hit on the head. During the whole of this rampage Inuee had never paid any attention to me (I honestly don't know why) but one of his wild slashes with the bayonet inadvertently struck the edge of my right hand inflicting a small cut which bled freely. During the whole of this unsavoury event the guards on duty made no attempt to stop it and, conversely, seemed to be enjoying it. Inuee then turned to me and instructed me to get Lieutenant Commander Upton and accompany him to a point just outside the main gate. Here he made us kneel down next to each other. I was wearing 'klompers' which I took off and kicked to one side. As we lowered ourselves to the ground he placed a bamboo rod in the angle behind our knees. Then with a sickening laugh he applied downward pressure to our shoulders. He repeated this several times and on each occasion the pain in both knees was excruciating. He then picked up one of my klompers and struck me on the forehead with it causing blood to run into my eyes. At the time I thought this may have damaged my eyes but it turned out that the cut was quite small and not too serious. The seriousness of this whole event cannot be overstated but there was an amusing part to it was well. After he had hit me over the head with the klomper, Inuee went over to the guardhouse, picked up a bottle of blue ink and poured it over the guard Commander's head. This, together with his sallow complexion, rendered his face a bright green. There was still more to come. Inuee then returned to me and commanded me to get up. He instructed me in perfect Japanese to bring out of the camp 'A man who looks like a woman'. A strange request and almost impossible to comply with. Which man would openly admit to looking like a woman and to even ask would be openly insulting. However, I had no choice. In camp was a black Dutch soldier called Billy Amour. He didn't look a bit effeminate but often played female parts in our stage productions. I plucked up courage and asked him. He declined. I then met the two cooks who were just coming off duty. I explained my predicament to them and to my surprise they both agreed. Now these two lads were built like brick shit-houses and weren't in the least bit effeminate. We walked back to the parade ground where, to my immense relief, everyone had gone, including Inuee.

Then came the process of treating the wounded. The MOs did the best they could.

Next morning Ebinuma told us that we were to receive a visit from Captain Myasaki from Camp 2. The time and purpose of his visit was uncertain. Was it related to the Inuee incident or was this just a co-incidence? Captain Armstrong had decided to 'hush-up' the whole incident. This did not please the Dutch. They wanted a 'show down' and nothing less. I understood Captain Armstrong's rationale. He feared reprisals from the Koreans and felt that an underlying reason was the uneasy relationship between the Japs and the Koreans. One aspect of the whole incident still bothered me. Why did Captain Armstrong escape injury despite being con-fronted by Inuee? Was it due to the rapport that the Captain had built up with the Koreans resulting in the latter having some respect for him? I don't know, but this certainly wouldn't help him in his bid to placate the Dutch as they were always suspicious of his relationship with the guards.

Anticipating Myasaki's visit, Captain Armstrong issued a camp order preventing any POW from leaving the camp until the visit was over. It got quite late and the visit still hadn't taken place so Captain Armstrong, believing that it wasn't going to happen, left the camp and went to the bathing area along with three fellow officers. Shortly after they had left, Myasaki arrived along with the Dutch interpreter M Kraal from Camp 2 and the Japanese doctor 1st Lieutenant Ishi. This was just what Captain Soeters wanted. He was second in command of the camp and was quick to exploit Captain Armstrong's absence. Ishi asked to see all those who had been injured in the incident. We all paraded and were examined by Ishi who was passing comments to Myasaki as he conducted his examination. The sequel to all this was a rapid visit by the Kempetai who took Inuee away for punishment.

As a footnote to this incident, I feel it is appropriate to draw attention to a book called 'Einde Station Pekanbaru' written by a Dutchman called Henk Hovinga. I have read this book and am conscious that other readers may also have read it. This incident is described in great detail on pages 101 and 102. Hovinga concludes by saying that the reason for Myasaki's visit was that Captain Armstrong had sent him a letter of complaint. This is categorically untrue. Following the visit Ebinuma confided in Captain Armstrong and I that Myasaki had visited as a direct result of a report made by the Japanese Medical Orderly Osaki. He was the only Japanese living in the Kebetai with the Koreans (must have been hell) and had witnessed the whole incident and felt obliged to report it to his boss 1st Lieutenant Ishi who wished to see the injuries for himself.

The Railway, when complete, would run between Pekanbaru and a place called Muaro. At Muaro it would join an existing eastbound line where this line met a branch line from the coal mines at Sawahlunto. The purpose of the line was to facilitate the transport of coal from the coal mines to Pekanbaru where it would then travel by river and sea to Singapore. It was being completed from both ends (Pekanbaru and Muaro) but the point of convergence had not yet been determined. We did hear that Camp 13 had opened at Muaro on 7 March 1945 so it appeared that progress was being maintained.

Life in camp continued as normal. The number of men required for outside working parties was mercifully reducing which was just as well because there was more than a corresponding increase in the number unavailable for work through sickness. Malaria, dysentery and beri-beri were ever present and the collective weakening effect over the past months was taking its toll. Ginger Woods continued with his work in the Kebetai and from time to time would return to camp with left over rice and veg. This was shared out equally and was a welcome treat when compared with our own basic fare. Similarly, from the guardroom, which was directly opposite my hut, the guard commander would occasionally shout 'Smissu meshi amari'.(Smith we have too much rice). I was never too proud to accept it. Food was always welcome, irrespective of the source, remember we were already eating snakes, rats, monkeys, cats and dogs. I would take the rice to Padre Rorke who would ensure that each POW got his fair share.

At the same time body lice, bed bugs and cockroaches were our constant companions. Most mornings you would wake up to find that any point of contact between body and bed had been bitten, but the offenders were nowhere to be seen. Shaven heads had helped to control body lice but the little blighters found other areas of the body to hatch out their progeny causing embarrassing itching and attention from the camp jokers. One night Ginger and I were sound asleep inside our mozzy net when I was wakened by some movement inside the net. It wasn't Ginger and it wasn't me. We had a visitor. It was a rat. It had fallen from one of the roof beams onto the mozzy net which was so worn that it went straight through it. In an attempt to find an escape route it crossed and re-crossed most parts of our bodies. We eventually eased the net out from under the bed mat to allow it to escape. That morning we mentioned to the MO Jock Macauley what had happened. He was most annoyed and said that we should have kept it for the 'pot'.

On 15 April 1945 we had our first death in Camp 3. It was Private AC Wales RAOC, aged 42 years. We had not met this situation before as the seriously ill POWs were usually transferred to Camp 2 where the medical facilities were slightly better. We designated an area of the camp as a graveyard. It wasn't a large area as we didn't want to be too pessimistic! As we had no coffins the deceased was wrapped in cane matting and interred. The last post was sounded and prayers were said. Irrespective of creed Padre Rorke always conducted the service if he was in camp. If not, there was never any shortage of volunteers to take his place. The behaviour of the Japanese on the occasion of any death was always respectful but a complete contradiction to their normal attitude towards POWs. We knew that their Shinto religion required them to worship their dead ancestors and they seemed to take this approach whenever a prisoner died. They would 'present arms' when a dead POW passed and if death occurred during a working party the Japs would always pay their respects along with the POWs comrades. They never prevented, hindered or interfered in the burial but could often be heard to say in Malay '*Orang mati bagus*'. (Good another dead one). Strange, and difficult to reconcile.

In late April drafts of POWs passed the camp by train en-route to Camp 7A. Their task was to rebuild the bridge over the Kampar Kiri River which had collapsed on 30 March (referred to earlier). The number of trains going up and down the line behind the camp increased significantly and we learnt that the Jap Railway Battalion was moving its workshops from Pekanbaru to Logas (eastwards towards Muaro at the other end of the line). But we were not sure what was happening? Was the line nearing completion? Was the war starting to turn against the Japs? It is fair to say that in all our time in captivity we learnt nothing about the progress of the war, particularly the war in Europe. We were starved of newspapers, radio was simply Japanese propaganda and any mail from home had been heavily censored. From time to time sympathetic natives would pass on information to working parties about the progress of the war but this was very sketchy and could never be confirmed. However, the natives had very recently suggested that the Germans had been defeated. We didn't believe it or didn't want to believe it but it turned out to be true. This, coupled with the increased activity of the Japs changed the mood in camp. Everyone felt that something significant was happening and it wasn't just the impending completion of the railway!

On 26 May a Dutch POW died. Another one died on 1June and another one on 12 June, bringing the total in the graveyard to four. On 22 June the second British POW died. He was Aircraftsman L Lewis, aged 23. On 9 July Aircraftsman JJ Stevenson died, aged 25. In the meantime three other Dutch POWs had died, so there were now nine graves. Six Dutch and three British.

The railway line from Muaro must have been making good progress in an easterly direction as the Japs closed Camp 14 and transferred all the POWs to Camp 7B at Lipatkain, Camp 9 at Logas and Camp 13 at Muaro. Camp 10 at Lubuk- Ambatjang was occupied in early July and on 12 July Camp 12 at Siloewah was occupied. It was clear that a completion date for the railway must be nearing.

Deaths in camp continued. Three more Dutch POWs (I'm sorry, I didn't record their names) and on 15 July an Australian called Foster died. The following day (16th) another Englishman, Gunner AE Rouse, died aged 41. July was a particularly demoralising month as on 25th another English POW died, Gunner LCJ Heard, RA, aged 38. This brought the number of dead to fifteen. Nine Dutch, five English and one Australian. By now the graveyard had been extended to accommodate the increasing number of dead.

We heard that the POWs at Camp 12 at Siloewah were now working round the clock on both day and night shifts and from a passing eastbound train we learnt that at Camp 9 at Logas the Jap Railway Technicians had informed the POWs that the railway would be completed on 15 August 1945. It was now 8 August so seven days for completion seemed very optimistic. A map showing the completed railway line is included at Appendix A

On 9 August another British POW died. He was Gunner WA Smith, aged 42.

At this time, Captain Armstrong and I asked Ebinuma for permission to buy a water buffalo to supplement our falling rations. To our delight he agreed and said that he would accompany us to make the purchase. One morning we set off early on foot. What a strange combination. A Japanese Officer, complete with sword, an English Army Captain, still slightly rotund, and a young Englishman. We walked past the lads working on the sand cliff and were subjected to some ribald comments. We hiked along the track sleeper to sleeper until it reached the jungle and shortly afterwards we followed Ebinuma down an embankment into the jungle. It was wet and boggy so we balanced on the trunks of fallen trees taking care not to fall into the waters below. Goodness knows what was in those waters? To Ebinuma's credit he appeared to know where he was going because soon we exited the jungle onto a hard mud road. The sweeping Kampar Kanan River was on our right and the mud road led us to a Kampong called Katabalu where a local ferry took us across the river. We met the Headman of the Kampong and Ebinuma and I explained to him that we wished to purchase one of his water buffaloes for cash. We bargained with the Headman for a while until a 'price' was agreed. I recall that we paid 1800 Japanese Guilders for the buffalo but have no idea what that might equate to in English currency. The water buffalo was presented to us and we put a rattan ring through its nostrils and an assembly of woven straw over its eyes. It was my job to lead it back to camp. Instead of returning to the jungle we had to follow the mud road. This increased the length of our journey as we had to pass the camp and then double back along the railway line. The buffalo wasn't entirely happy and had to be restrained as I'm sure it could smell the water in the nearby jungle where it would have been more 'at home'. On the return journey Ebinuma kept referring to the money we had provided to effect the purchase. We just changed the subject as we realised he was having difficulty reconciling the amount we had paid with the wages we were given for our work in camp. In truth, the disparity was made up from the illicit trading in the jungle by Dave Spero and Paddy Davin. Fortunately Ebinuma didn't pursue his questioning so we made him no wiser. The open aspect of the mud road offered no protection from the noon-day sun so we were relieved to reach camp. We tethered the buffalo on a piece of spare ground and ate some welcome rice pap (porridge). We had just settled down when we heard quite a commotion. The buffalo had broken free from its tether and, still with its blinkers on, had made its way into a paddy field where it submerged so that only its nostrils were visible. Some of the more knowledgeable Dutch Colonial soldiers observed that it was 'in-calf' so it wouldn't have been slaughtered anyway. The Headman eventually recovered the buffalo and it was agreed that we would re-visit him in the future to collect another one.

On 18 August another POW died. He was Private WT Fraser, an Australian aged 41.

Chapter Six

The Japs surrender – preparing for freedom

We now reached a point where our earlier suspicions relating to the progress of the war were beginning to gather momentum. The rumour machine was working overtime. One of the Korean guards mentioned that he had heard that Russian Troops had entered the north of Korea. At the same time we received official confirmation that the railway had in fact been completed. This was on 15 August 1945. The two lines had converged at a place called Pintu Batu near Camp 11. The Japs had held a ceremony and presented themselves with medals.

There was definitely something going on. It was rumoured that all POWs were being transferred to Singapore. Next there was a rumour that five additional barrack huts were to be built at Camp 3 and on 20 August an order was issued by the Japs that from the next day our daily rice ration was to be increased from 350gms to 600gms and other rations increased accordingly. Vegetables were to be provided daily and proper meat (instead of entrails and bones) was to be provided every sixth day. All the Korean guards were given an advance in rank and had been ordered to be kinder towards the POWs and not employ them as Tobans. It was still not certain why we had been subjected to this sudden rush of kindness. Was it reward for completing the railway or was there some other reason? The rumour that Russians had entered Korea may have been a clue. There was certainly a more positive mood in camp, not exactly euphoria, as yet another British POW died. He was Aircraftsman A Moore, aged 40. We now had twenty graves in the graveyard. Eleven Dutch, seven English and two Australian.

22 August started just like any other day and the camp routine continued as normal. However, that night Kobayashi (King Kong) called me and said that he wished to speak to Captain Armstrong and me in the POW kitchen after Tenko. We met as requested and because we were in the kitchen were joined by Lieutenant Chadwick the Kitchen Officer. Kobayashi was noticeably nervous which was completely out of character. He kept looking over his shoulder to check if we were still alone. He said 'Hanashimasu hemitsu' (we must speak secretly). He then said 'Hewa narumashita'. This translates as 'Peace has become'. I translated this to Captain Armstrong and Lieutenant Chadwick and will never forget the expression on their faces as they digested it. They never spoke but I feel their thoughts were one of total disbelief. Kobayashi then shook hands with all three of us. A strange situation as he was probably the most brutal of the Gunsoku. He then went on to say that Korea was to become independent from Japan after many years of occupation and that the Japanese had signed an armistice on 19 August and all members of the Nippon government had been told to commit 'Hari-kiru' by the Emperor. He also said that because he was Korean he was not sure what his

position was. Finally, agreeing to keep the whole discussion private he departed, leaving all three of us seated and reflecting on what we had just heard. Shortly after his departure Kobayashi's motive dawned on us. He was trying to curry favour with us by playing the 'good guy'. Because he was Korean his position was uncertain and he obviously feared reprisals from the POWs because of the way he had behaved towards them. That night I couldn't sleep. My thoughts turned to Penrith. I saw myself walking along Middlegate outside Robinson's Infant School. The more I tried to get off to sleep the more my thoughts turned to Penrith. I was repeating this same journey along Middlegate passing the Alhambra Cinema. The activity in my brain was surpassing my natural tiredness. I was on edge and saw that outside it was a bright moonlit night (not unusual in the tropics) so I nudged Ginger who was sleeping like a log next to me. He eventually woke and after much huffing, puffing and rubbing of eyes said' *What's up?'* I said '*Follow me*'. We went outside and sat on a disused ant-hill close to the barrack. By now he was fully awake. I said to him '*The war is over*'. Please excuse the language but his reply went something like this '*What the fuck are you talking about? Have you gone off your bloody rocker? Don't be so bloody daft'. Let's get some fucking shut-eye*'. I asked him to keep it secret and we returned to our mozzy net and I fell into a genuine deep sleep. Obviously getting the matter off my chest was the safety valve I was looking for and prompts a quote from Robert Browning–

There, that is our secret: go to sleep!
You will wake, and remember, and understand.

The next day news began to trickle into camp about a possible Jap surrender. It gathered traction so that I was constantly approached by the more inquisitive POWs and asked '*What's going on?*' Obviously, I had to reply that I didn't know but they would say '*Come on, we're not bloody daft you know*'. That same day Ginger went as usual to do his work at the Kebetai but hadn't been away long before he came to me 'brimming over' with observations. '*Yes, something is afoot. The Koreans are busy sorting out their kit and destroying paper-work*'. I think he now believed me! That evening Kanimitsu (he got the M&B tablets for Captain Armstrong) came to see me. He presumed that I knew what was going on as he said that the war was not offi-cially over (which raised some doubt in my mind) but went on to say that all the guards had been paid four months wages in one payment without explaining why. He also said that three cases of medical supplies had been delivered to our camp and the delivery driver had informed him that new clothing for POWs (which had been requisitioned earlier) had arrived at Camp 2. Also 80 tons of rice from the ration centre at Bankinan was due to arrive for distribution. That day I also received five letters from home all of which had been consider-ably delayed. (I will mention this in more detail later).

There was still no official confirmation of the Jap surrender so a feeling of great uncertainty prevailed. The Koreans were playing an interesting and clever game. They had packed their kit bags ready for any sub-sequent order but were now being exceptionally friendly towards the POWs. Clearly they were in a difficult and unenviable position. They were hated by the Japs who saw them as inferior. They in turn hated the Japs as they saw them as conquerors. They were also hated by the POWs because of their brutal behaviour towards them. We concluded that their 'end game' was to achieve a transfer from the 'losing' side to the 'winning' side. We were in an equally difficult position as the Japs and, therefore, the Koreans were effectively still in charge despite all that had happened recently. So, on our part it was reasonable to accommodate the Korean's friendliness without being too patronising. In any case, Captain Armstrong had always fostered a fatherly relationship with them which paid dividends in the current climate. Our fear was the Dutch. They certainly didn't agree with Captain Armstrong's approach and, perhaps, more importantly saw the Japs as invaders of what was once their territory, unlike the Allied troops who had no real affinity with the area. Our fear was that they would try to assert their authority too soon and start something over which they had (as yet) no control. So we watched them carefully for any signs of aggression.

The change in attitude continued. Ebinuma came into camp. Something never previously experienced. He wanted Captain Armstrong and I to accompany him to Katabulu Kampong the next day to get another buffalo to replace the escapee. Without being asked! Unheard of before! The events of that evening, 24 August 1945 will stick in my mind forever. I remember them as if they happened yesterday and can claim that I never, ever thought I would find myself in such a position.

The Korean Guard Commander approached me and 'requested' not 'ordered' me to accompany Captain Armstrong to Ebinuma's house. We were greeted by Ebinuma who had also requested the attendance of Captain Soeters, the senior Dutch officer. Almost immediately after our arrival the door opened and who should enter but the dreaded Captain Myasaki the Senior Japanese Officer (he was based at Camp 2). I had only met him once before when he came to deal with the aftermath of Inuee's rampage. It was 6.40pm. He looked very stern. His brutal reputation always preceded him. I had no reason to change my mind but wasn't intimidated by his presence. Naturally, he took centre stage. Nervously, he read from a paper written in Nipponese which he held in front of him. He read it out in short statements which I was required to interpret. It interprets as follows-

The Nipponese armed forces have, under orders from Tenno Heika and The High Government of Nippon, ceased to carry on the war and as from 14 August 1945 arranged a state of armistice. It is my wish that the camps shall continue, so far as possible, as before. I shall leave all responsibility, as before, ably in the hands of the various Camp Commanders (1,2,3,6&7). I recommend friendship with the guards, remembering that they are an inferior nationality, until such time as an allied delegation shall come here to Sumatra and I must hand over the prisoners. I do not want any untoward incidents with the prisoners who must keep within bounds. I shall do everything in my power to obtain extra rations whenever possible. The sick people must be well cared for and restored to health to enable them to go home fit and well. The people that have died, their relatives will be informed that they passed away peacefully and any belongings that are left, take them along also. The graves must also be kept clean and tidy. Lastly, I wish to thank you one and all for the way in which we have worked together.'

This was followed by hand shaking all round and Myasaki, obviously relieved to have delivered his message, left very quickly. Then complete silence as those present tried to assimilate what had just been said. Whilst the message was most welcome its hypocrisy and insincerity made it difficult to swallow. It would be interesting to see how the Dutch reacted to it!

At 7.30pm a general parade was held and the message delivered to the assembled POWs. First in English and then Dutch. Both National Anthems were sung, followed by a short silence for those 'no longer with us'. The parade was then dismissed.

Later Wing Commander Davis, the Senior POW Commander approached Myasaki in an attempt to get a definitive statement. Myasaki wouldn't admit that the Japs had capitulated simply repeating his previous statement that 'a cease fire had been declared'. This didn't deter the Wing Commander who returned to camp and said *The war is over* which was a much more positive message for the POWs. He then ordered the musicians playing in the sick bay to strike up both national anthems.

Events in all the other camps followed a similar pattern. Out on the railway line the Japs had said, *'No more hard work, no more beatings and much yasume'*.

Meals were improving and the guard's friendly approach continued. At Camp 2 nothing more was forthcoming from Myasaki and news from the natives dried up as they feared reprisals from the Japs. Myasaki continued to use his authority to control the camps. In the meantime at Camp 2 which was the Jap HQ, Myasaki, assisted by Lieutenant Doi, Sergeant Major Igari, Sergeant Major Aika and Sergeant Shinomara set about burning all documentation and archives.

The mood in camp changed significantly. No more saluting or bowing to the guards. POWs could walk in and out of the camp as never before. The Korean guards kept coming into camp shaking hands and giving their greetings. They declared that their position was still uncertain. Later that evening Kunimoto, Hirowka and Kanida invited all the Dutch and British 'Staff' for a roast chicken supper in the POW kitchen.

The next day the Koreans were still on guard but were all wearing brand new uniforms. The previous day the Japs had searched their belongings and removed certain items. Ebinuma arrived in camp and Captain Armstrong and I accompanied him to the Kampong to buy two buffalo bullocks to replace the escapee. When we got back to camp we were invited by the Koreans to drink sake with them. Their hospitality was now getting a bit over the top. Nevertheless, they were still in charge so we complied. Later Mitsui came to walk and talk with me and, although he never broached the subject directly, it was clear he was worried about what was going to happen to him and his colleagues. That day we were told to place a large 'PW' sign on the football field for sighting by aircraft. 200gms of fresh fish were delivered along with some planks, clothes and cigarettes.

At half past four the next morning I was woken by Naraiya, one of the Duty Guards. He asked me to get Captain Armstrong and the Dutch MO (sorry, his name eludes me – he was the tapeworm expert) and meet him at the back of the camp. It was quite misty and when we arrived we saw that a table had been laid (at this unearthly hour) with sake, boiled meat, salt and cigarettes. We sat in the moonlight and were joined by Nihida and Miyama. The discussion inevitably turned to their current position. They wanted to know whether we were 'for' or 'against' them. We were very non-committal. We went to bed at 5.30am very tired.

That day there was another death. A Dutch soldier called F vanDijk aged 48. He had died from beri-beri.

Breakfast was fried fresh fish which was a luxury when compared with previous ones. I was issued with a new white shirt, shorts, fundoshi and towel. Things were definitely improving.

On 29 August there were two more deaths. Bombardier M Vallance RA, aged 38 and a Dutch soldier called JC Rondeau, aged 42. Any death was a sad occasion but to die when freedom was in sight was particularly upsetting. That day the Dutch Commanding Officer in Camp 2, Lieutenant Colonel Slabbekoorn, instructed that a party from Camp 3 should go to the old flooded Camp 3 to exhume the body of Dutch Sergeant Major Meyer who had died in August 1944 at Katabalu and been buried there. His body was brought back to Camp 3 and re-interred. I was aware that a British POW, Bombardier Sergeant Roy, had also been buried alongside the Dutch Sergeant Major but his body was never exhumed and re-interred and couldn't understand why. On my return home I made enquiries of a Dutch exPOW who told me that Roy had his own grave outside Camp 3. In 1988 I wrote to the British War Graves Commission regarding this. They were very helpful but informed me that they had no trace of this man.

Also on 29 August the Koreans ceased to guard the camp. They were stripped of their rifles and equipment which was sent to Camp 2. Six rifles were then issued to our Camp and we mounted our own guard on a rota basis. One day British, two days Dutch, to commence on 1 September.

On 30th fifty POWs arrived from Camp 2 on a temporary basis and Kobayashi (him again) informed me that an agreement had been signed by the Japs ending the war and that Korea was now independent. Another Dutch POW died. He was Sergeant Major Jalhay aged 51.

The 31st was the Dutch Queen's birthday so a parade was held on the football field and the Dutch flag was hoisted. In the evening the Koreans threw yet another party. It was in the Nippon kitchen. Invited were Captain Armstrong, Lieutenant Chadwick, Lieutenant Dallas and myself. We were the guests of Miyama (we argued about Auld Lang Syne) and Harada. We had an enjoyable evening. Although we weren't aware at the time it was their 'leaving' party as they were all shipped out next day to an exclusively Korean camp at Kilometre 3.

On the evening of 1 September Captain Armstrong, Captain Soeters, De Jong, the Dutch Interpreter and I were invited to Ebinuma's house. We ate Suki-yaki and had a farewell drink with him. He was quite overcome with emotion. He asked Captain Soeters and De Jong to leave which they did. He then surrendered his ceremonial sword to Captain Armstrong. An extremely touching moment despite all that had gone before. We then left and on the way back to camp we reflected on Ebinuma's character and behaviour whilst he had been our camp Commandant. He was unlike previous Commandants. He was approachable and quite humane in comparison. He had done his best to protect the POWs from the excessive demands of the Railway Engineers and had accommodated most of our requests whenever possible. For example, he allowed us to purchase the buffalo. We felt that he knew that the money we used for the purchase was illicit but chose to ignore it. We agreed, therefore, that it would be appropriate to provide Ebinuma with a letter of 'safe conduct' highlighting his compassionate nature and kindness towards the POWs. Our rationale may have been misplaced but we sincerely hoped that it may prove beneficial to Ebinuma should he ever appear before a War Crimes Commission. I prepared the letter with guidance from Captain Armstrong and we handed it to Ebinuma. We explained its purpose and he accepted it with a deep bow and a final handshake. I can reveal here that after the war he spent time in Changi Jail in Singapore eventually appearing before a War Crimes Commission in May 1947 in Singapore. Like most other Camp Commanders he expected to be sentenced to death. In fact he was released and repatriated to Japan and I subsequently learnt from his family that he believed the letter had saved his life. Letters dated 21 August and 1 September 1952 received from Ebinuma are reproduced in the Epilogue at pages 225 and 226.

On 5 September yet another British POW died. He was Gunner GG Carrington, aged 38 who died of beriberi. The graveyard which began in April now had 25 graves. 14 Dutch, 9 British and 2 Australians.

On 6 September I was issued with a pink Wan-sho (armband) which allowed me to leave the camp and go to Camp 2 which was our Headquarters. I met many of my old acquaintances. I visited the hospital and the cemetery. I also had an interview with Wing Commander Davis who by now was a very busy man. He thanked me for my services as interpreter and also gave me access to the total number of deaths up to the present time. I recorded these as follows –

Dutch (incl Colonials) - 431
British   - 204
Australian   - 38
American   - 3
Norwegian   - 1
Total   - 677

Some 27,000 Romushas had also died and 6,000 of these had actually died in the hospital at Simpang Tiga.

On 7 September the ration wagon driver (always a good source of news) told us that at 1am a British Major called Lodge had arrived at Camp 2. He was a Commando and part of a 'recce' party which had been secretly dispatched to Sumatra to assess the position of the POWs and to try and make contact with the Japanese High Command. He had arrived in a small fishing Kampong called Bagan Siapiapi on the north east coast of Sumatra some two months previously. I will provide more detail of this operation later but on his visit to Camp 2 he did say that Lord Mountbatten had been in Singapore for the last few days and had expressed his annoyance at the conditions in which the POWs and other internees were being kept. Later that day two large Aircraft flew over the camp heading in a north westerly direction. The first we had seen in three and a half years. We were ordered to remove the PW sign from the football field as it may not be suitable for 'dead drops' (drops without parachute). We were also informed that on the day that the Allies re-occupied Singapore our King had said that he and the Queen were aware of the hardships that POWs were enduring under the Japanese and the thoughts of all back home were with us. He went on to say that everything possible would be done to help us and the Officer Commanding Singapore would get us all on our way as soon as ships were available. He finished by saying that all he heard from POWs was *'We want to go back home'*. We also heard that two atomic bombs had been dropped on Tokyo causing devastation and thousands of casualties? This did bear out what Kobayashi had told me previously. He said *'Ni no okino bakudon Nihon'*. (Two very big bombs on Japan). I hadn't given him credit for his accuracy and had forgotten about it until now. I think it is important to record that after the war had ended the Allies recovered Japanese Military Orders which confirmed beyond all doubt that if the impending landing of Allied Invasion Troops was to take place then all POWs and Romushas had to be eliminated. Similar Orders were recovered in Bangkok confirming this. Thus every surviving POW will quickly affirm that the two bombs, as dreadful as they were, undoubtedly saved our lives despite what the 'doubters' and pacifists might say. (It is still controversial to this day).

Another interesting point is that before the secret infiltration of the island by the Allies nothing was known about the Trans Sumatra railway, quite simply because it was outside any battle area. On the other hand the Burma railway was well known to the Allies. The Americans had gathered this information from survivors of ships torpedoed by the Japs en-route to Japan from Singapore. So the secret infiltration parties were surprised at what they found and when the extent of the problem was radioed back to Allied Command they were completely shocked. Hence, commentators subsequently referred to it as 'The Forgotten Railway'.

On 8 September another Dutch POW died. He was CJ Khim aged 52. This was the sixth death since the end of the war. That morning we received some very important visitors. Wing Commander Davis, Major Lodge (referred to earlier), Major GF Jacobs, Royal Marines, a Dutch interpreter and seven Japanese Officers including a Lieutenant Colonel and two Captains. Major Jacobs took lots of photographs especially of those POWs suffering from beri-beri and malnutrition. Major Jacobs had also led a 'recce' party like Major Lodge. He then delivered a speech which I summarise as follows –

He was aware of the conditions in which we had been held and that plans were already in place for the delivery of essentials such as medicine, clothes and food. These would be brought by air from Ceylon (now Sri Lanka) and parachuted, firstly to those areas in greatest need, and then to others. Delivery by ship was impossible at present as all harbours and the Malacca Straits had been mined by the Japanese. Clothes were the heaviest items so these would be left to last. Newspapers would also be provided to allow us to 'get back to normal' as quickly as possible. A special study of our diet had been completed so the food provided would be what the researchers felt was most required. He also mentioned that the sudden change in diet carried a risk of stomach upsets and the like. Every effort was being made to establish a system for mail to be sent home. In the meantime all nominal rolls would be recorded and radioed back to the War Ministry to allow families to be informed. The sick would be taken away by air ambulance to hospitals in India once the airfield at Pekanbaru had been made serviceable. All POWs considered 'fit' would go home directly to the UK as soon as the ships arrive. He went on to say that it takes 16 hours for a plane to fly from Ceylon and that you (the POWs) must become accustomed to the fact the world is a nice place to live in even though the last three and a half years might suggest otherwise.

He then went to inspect the hospital and kitchen along with the Japanese. He then took some more photographs before leaving to inspect Camp 9 at Logas.

In the early 1950s I was able to contact Major Jacobs in South Africa. I asked him if it was possible to have copies of the photos he took whilst in Camp 3. He duly obliged and these are produced below.

This photo was taken outside barrack No 2. From the left is Ginger Woods, myself, AN Other, 'Chiefy' Thomas, D Fogarty,? Nicholls, AN Other, MA Rees, GM Hull MO.

Taken outside barrack No 3. In the centre with the white arm band is Wing Commander Davis, Senior POW Officer, talking to the Dutch Captain. The building on the extreme right is the 'Dedek' factory where vitamin serum for intra-venous injection was produced.

That evening some more supplies were delivered. Two packets of 'Koa' cigarettes, one packet of tooth-powder and one toothbrush for each POW.

At 6pm on the 9th a four- engined aircraft circled the camp and then flew away towards Pekanbaru but quickly returned at a lower altitude over Simpang Tiga and dropped five parachutes. It circled three more times and then flew away. The parachutists were two RAMC Captains, one RAMC Sergeant Orderly, one Major and one Flight Lieutenant. The following day we assembled for a 'news' parade. The 'news' had come from the parachutists. Within ten to fourteen days we would be on the move. They had also brought medicines resulting in us all receiving an anti-malaria injection and multi vitamin tablets. MOs had to prepare returns of POWs in the following categories to facilitate recovery: Category A – fit for transport to the UK by ship. Category B – Convalescent but on a 'diet'. Category C – Ambulatory cases. Category D – Hospital ship. Category E – Requiring further hospitalisation before repatriation. Category F – Dangerously ill.

In the early afternoon an RAF Liberator passed over the camp at a good height, turned in the direction of the sports field and suddenly released a single parachute with a long torpedo shaped canister attached. It floated off target and landed between the Guardroom and Vegetable plot. The next pass over the camp was much lower and this time the plane made some 'dead drops' consisting of bundles of newspapers and sacks of dried beans and peas. The plane then made a really low pass over the camp. The side door was wide open and three of the crew were leaning out and waving. The canister had been packed with goods jointly from HM Force, the British Red Cross and St John War Organisation. Notably, it contained 'Jungle rations' including instructions for their use. (Produced below).

The most novel item was the milk in a tube. Many POWs thought this was toothpaste and ended up with a mouthful of milk. There were razors, towels, biscuits, tinned food, soup, sewing equipment, sugar, salt, cigarettes, hair brushes and combs. By the way, hair had now re-grown so the latter items would be useful. The canister also contained the following message –

Sept '45. 357 Squadron RAF Ceylon. Hello Gang. Sorry we can't put more and better things in the parcels but it is just what we could grab in a hurry. We hope

THE JUNGLE RATION (MARK II) (A.L.)

SUGGESTED MENU

BREAKFAST	POCKET MEAL	SUPPER
Meat or Fish (a) *	4 biscuits.	Meat (b) * (separate pack).
Porridge (2 oatmeal blocks).		3 biscuits.
3 biscuits.	2 bars chocolate.	Cheese.
Tea (half quantity provided).		Tea (half quantity provided).
Jam.	Boiled sweets.	

Also included:—Milk (in tube), I extra bar of chocolate, I packet chewing gum, I packet salt, 4 tablets sugar, I packet fizz tablets, matches, latrine paper, 30 salt tablets, I compound vitamin tablet.

*NOTE (a) Ham and Egg, or Fish and Egg, or Chopped Liver and Bacon, or Breakfast Pork.

(b) Meat Preserved, or Stewed Steak, or Meat and Kidney Pudding, or Chopped Ham and Beef, or equivalent item.

METHOD OF PREPARATION

1. PORRIDGE

Crumble oatmeal block finely into mess tin with the aid of jack knife. Add sufficient water to make thin paste. Cook for 4-5 minutes, stirring the whole time, and adding more water if porridge becomes too thick.

2. TEA

Fill mess tin with about I pint of water. Bring to boil. Crumble half the quantity of tea tablets provided and throw into boiling water and stir once or twice. Continue boiling for a moment, and allow to stand for a few minutes so that the leaves can sink to the bottom of the mess tin. Add milk and sugar as required.

J.8737 1466 18336/5497 1,000,000 6/44 C.P. Ltd. Gp. 9.8.2.

[PLEASE TURN OVER

NOTES

1. If circumstances make cooking impossible, the oatmeal blocks may be eaten dry, in which case :—

    (a) Eat them slowly.

    (b) Chew them well.

    (c) Drink some water at the same time or soon after.

2. The chocolate may be made into a palatable drink by breaking into small pieces and cooking in half a pint of water.

3. The fizz tablets (three tablets to half a pint of water) will make a refreshing drink. Do not drink until the tablets are completely dissolved.

4. The salt tablets will prevent you from becoming a casualty to the heat. One tablet should be taken with every pint of water that you drink.

5. It is most important that you should swallow the Compound Vitamin tablet every day. Your health and strength will suffer if you do not.

[PLEASE TURN OVER

that the reading matter will pass a few hours for most of you. Our greatest hope and prayers are that before many days are past you will all be heading home. Best of luck. We remain - Ernie Mercer, Skipper (Canada), Flight Sergeant Phillips, Second Pilot (England), F MacKelvie, Navigator (Canada). KE Duff, Bomb Aimer (Canada). PF Astle, Air Gunner (Canada). GC Bale, Wireless/Air Gunner (Canada). T Pattinson (Canada). J Beirnes (Canada) and J Bower (England).

On the 11th a further death occurred. This time it was a Dutch civilian called Fillekes, aged 44. This brought the total graves to 28 (7 since the end of the war). All POWs received an anti- cholera injection and in the newspapers we read that an Australian captain speaking on behalf of General Blamey at the re-occupation of New Guinea had said of the Japs '*I can no longer regard you as an honourable enemy. Your conduct during the occupation of these islands and your treatment of POWs is far below that of a civilized nation*'. Also we read that the joint operation of HM Services and the Red Cross would be re-named Repatriation Allied Prisoners of War and Internees (RAPWI) under the overall command of Brigadier Lloyd (Australia) based in Colombo, Ceylon.

I mentioned earlier, but very briefly, that the Japanese Area Commander had for some cruel reason been holding back Red Cross boxes and mail from the POWs. This was discovered after the Japs had capitulated and a warehouse at the Commanders Headquarters was searched and found to contain consignments of mail intended for distribution to the POWs. Inspection of the mail showed that between posting in the UK and being received a period ranging from 12 to 22 months had elapsed. The Allies took possession of it and arranged for it to be distributed. Sadly there were letters or cards for those POWs who had since died. Up to now I had received nine lots of mail as follows: 15 January 1944 one letter dated June 1942. 2 October 1944 six letters dated April to June 1943. 26 October 1944 seven letters dated February to July 1943. 24 November 1944 one letter (the one handed to me by Nagai). 2 January 1945 three letters dated February and March 1944. 7 January 1945 nine letters dated February 1943 to May 1944. 20 January 1945 eight letters dated April to November 1943. 22 January 1945 four letters dated July 1943 to January 1944 and finally on 24 August 1945 four letters dated August 1944 to October 1944. Even allowing for the distance and circumstances under which this mail was to be delivered the receipt of my mail highlights not only the considerable delay but also the erratic nature of distribution. If this wasn't bad enough it turns out that mail in the opposite direction was just as bad, if not worse. This mail was routed via Russia, Portugal and Switzerland but the Japanese High Command was most unwilling to co-operate with the neutral authorities. This meant that next of kin had been virtually starved of information relating to their loved ones. In my case, I sent a letter by Clipper Air Mail on 1 December 1941 (before capture) which was received by my parents on 27 January 1942. But after that my parents heard nothing. To their eternal credit, they never lost faith and without exception they wrote and sent a letter or card every Sunday. In June and July 1942, to their obvious disappointment, nine letters and three cards were returned marked 'Return to sender, no service available'. In July 1942 my father wrote to the

RAF Records Office in an attempt to ascertain if I was still alive and, if so, my whereabouts. He received a reply dated 3 August 1942 stating that they had no information as to my circumstances. This letter is reproduced at Appendix B. On 16 March 1943 my parents received a telegram from the Air Ministry in London stating (for the first time) that I was a POW in Japanese hands. Thus they had the agonising wait of some 15 months (1 December 1941 to March 1943) before learning that I was still alive. The telegram stated that a letter would follow. This letter dated 15 March 1943 arrived on 17 March 1943 and stated that I was in captivity in 'Java Camp'. On 14 April 1943 a similar letter was received from the British Red Cross. These communications are also included at Appendix B. The Japs did allow us to send postcards from time to time. The content was limited to four set phrases and a few words of your own. The cards were purposely undated so that there was no indication of how long they had been in transit. An example is included at Appendix B. It was received by my parents on 24 September 1945 (after the armistice) and I guess I would send it some time between July and November 1944. From the text you will see that I said 'Not so hot as Java' in the hope that my parents would realise that I had moved. I was not allowed to indicate Sumatra.

On 12 September two more Dutch POWs died from beri-beri. They were F van Leent, aged 40 and FC Pieters, aged 51. This brought the total to 30. 19 Dutch, 9 British and 2 Australians. Thankfully, I can report that these were the last. After the war the bodies of all POWs were exhumed and transferred to the military cemeteries in Java. The Dutch went to Leuwigadjah at

Cimahi. The British to Menteng Pulu on the outskirts of Jakarta. I mentioned earlier that I returned to Indonesia in 1988 (I stood on the railway station at Tasikmalaya where I was captured) and took the opportunity to visit the cemetery at Menteng Pulu. It is managed by the War Graves Commission and was in immaculate condition. I found the graves of all the British POWs whose funerals I had attended in Camp 3 at Kubang between April and September 1945. Each grave had been carefully tended. I took a photograph of each one. These are re-produced at Appendix C

One of the advantages of writing these memoirs a long time after the actual events is that I can provide more detail and can claim that my narrative is accurate and not based on conjecture or supposition. So please allow me to put a little more definition on the Allied Infiltration of Sumatra. The operation was controlled from Ceylon (now Sri Lanka) and had commenced well before the cessation of hostilities. In the early stages six Secret Reconnaissance Parties had landed on Sumatra but they all failed to return. This was followed by further 'landings' including Majors Lodge and Jacobs. They were all equipped with radio transmitters and operated under a secret code. Major Lodge at Pekanbaru was 'Steel'. Major Jacobs at Medan was 'Arrest'. Major Lodge's party was made up of Chinese soldiers. Lam Kie Tjhong (Tiger). Lo Djoen Tjhin (Cyclops) and Lo Djoen Tjhin (Jackass). Major Jacob's party was made up of two Australian Sergeants Baites and Gillam, a Dutch Sergeant Plesman and a Chinese Lie TjieTjoeng. At this time the Japanese had agreed an armistice so one of the roles of these 'parties' was to try and establish contact with the Japanese High Command on the island to ensure that the terms of the armistice were adhered to. One of the terms was that the Japs would remain in charge of all POWs until Allied Forces were in a position to take over. The overall situation that prevailed was quite delicate, to say the least. Many natives and not a few POWs were keen to settle old scores with the Japs and a further dimension was the deep and incensed feeling that many natives had towards the Dutch having been exploited for many years under their Colonial rule. Whilst occupying the former Dutch East Indies the Japs had promoted 'Asia for the Asians' furthering the resolve of the natives never again to submit to the rule of the Dutch on their islands. One incident that highlights this delicate situation occurred in Medan when a native mob attacked an Internment Camp believing the occupants to be Dutch. They were in fact Swiss and, therefore, completely neutral but it resulted in twenty men, women and children being slaughtered. Lodge and Jacobs had been briefed not to get involved in politics but this was difficult because they also had to listen to the demands of all interested groups. Despite this, they knew that their priority was the welfare and repatriation of the POWs so it was paramount that they got to the Japanese High Command as quickly as possible. This task was handed to Major Jacobs. He realised that once this contact was established it would require the very best in International Diplomacy. He knew that he was hopelessly outnumbered (there were still some 80,000 Japanese soldiers on Sumatra) and the only bargaining tool he possessed was the impending arrival of the Allied troops. He still didn't know when/if, who and how many would be arriving. Neither did the Japs. He ascertained that the Jap High Command was located in

Medan (ironically where he had first landed). His team arrived in Medan and booked into the largest hotel The Hotel de Boer. Using the hotel switchboard he got his Chinese Malay speaking telegraphist to contact the Jap HQ. This he did and asked to be put through to an English speaking Jap Officer. Jacobs and the officer then spoke. Jacobs said he was an Allied Officer with the authority to contact the Jap High Command. The Jap response was rather obtuse as they suggested he could be an impersonator. He then said '*Well come and see for yourselves*'. The reply was '*Where we find you?*' He explained and their response was '*We send men to look*'. In an attempt to assert his authority Jacobs replied '*Don't keep us long*'.

They duly arrived. There was a Captain and a number of soldiers from the Kempetai secret police. Jacobs insisted that he must 'go to the top' and speak to the General. There were long periods of silence and a game of cat and mouse ensued which seemed to rest on who was to visit who. Jacobs stood his ground much to the Jap Captain's displeasure but the meeting eventually took place on Jacob's terms. The Jap Officer was Colonel Okada, Chief Staff Officer of the 2nd Imperial Division. He was accompanied by Major Imamura. Jacobs was keen to quickly gain their trust as without this the rest of his mission would fail. After a series of meetings the Japanese resistance finally mellowed, probably as a result of their own HQ vouching for Jacobs. Once he had their co-operation Jacobs requested the location and number of all POWs and internees and insisted that he still had to make contact with the General. Sumatra is a large island and travel by road was difficult and slow so Jacobs pushed his hand and ordered the Japs to provide an aircraft and pilot for his use. To his surprise they agreed and realising that the Japs were renowned for their kamikaze suicide pilots he insisted that they also provide an Officer and interpreter to accompany him. Colonel Yoshida and his interpreter Captain Sodi joined Jacobs and with a Jap pilot flew to Bukit Tinggi (formerly Fort de Kock). They then travelled by car to a municipal building in the township where they had a face to face meeting with General Tenabe the Officer Commanding Sumatra. After nervous introductions Jacobs informed Tenabe that he was the bearer of authority from the Supremo Lord Louis Mountbatten and repeated the terms of the armistice so far as they affected the Japanese. Jacobs pushed his hand yet again demanding a better plane from Tenabe to allow him to continue his journeys. This was supplied and Jacob flew to Padang and then Medan. Here he learnt in secret that there was a considerable amount of unrest from the Freedom Party and now the Communist Party. Like most they were unsure what was happening and both insisted that they would not make a move until the Allies had landed on the island and that the Occupation Forces would not be Dutch.

Jacobs, Yoshida and Sodi then flew to Pekanbaru where they began their initial visits to Camps 2 and 3 (I mentioned this visit earlier). The visit to Camp 2 allowed Jacobs to obtain the facts and figures he required and these were radioed back to Ceylon. At the same time Jacobs suspected that Yoshida had not come clean and that there could be other POW and Internee camps that he hadn't declared. He then had a stand up row with Yoshida and confronted him over the issue. Yoshida then declared one more camp and apologised, claiming it was an oversight. Jacobs was most annoyed as this had not been included in his report to HQ. The camp turned out to be a woman's camp at Loebeck Linggau. Jacobs insisted that he and Yoshida should visit the camp immediately. They flew to the nearest airstrip at Lahat. What they found was atrocious. There were about 1,000 women and children living under the most awful conditions.

In conclusion, the importance and dangerous nature of the work undertaken by Majors Jacobs and Lodge and their teams (and other teams who I haven't mentioned)) cannot be overstated. They played a most crucial role in the safety and repatriation of POWs who were eternally indebted to them.

All POWs received a personal memorandum from Lord Mountbatten which read as follows-

'I have given instructions that, as the surrender of all Japanese Forces has been accomplished, first priority must be given to bringing to you the help that you need. As soon as we can reach your camps arrangements will be made to get you home. But you must remember that many camps are so far away that it will be some time before we can reach you. Until we do and until our shipping, designed for the invasion of Malaya, can be re-deployed I shall see that you get all possible help, supplies and news from home. Arrangements are being made to inform your relatives at once that you are safe and at liberty. This has been a long war but from the time that you fell into enemy hands you have never been forgotten either in England or among the armies that have defeated the Japanese. I hope that it will now be only a matter of weeks at most before you are on your way home'.

On 15th there was a lot of aerial activity. Three RAF Officer Pilots called at Camp 3 and told us that 100 patients had been flown to Singapore that very day. We had many questions for them which they endeavoured to answer. One of them, a Flight Lieutenant Anderson had a brilliant idea. He took the names and addresses of all the remaining POWs and said he would try and get a message to our families back home. Reproduced below is the actual message received by my parents on 2 October 1945. He had sent the list of names and addresses to his wife who then took the trouble to send this message to the relatives of everyone on the list. Marvellous!

```
                              Kilsae,
                                 Oswald Av.,
                                    Grangemouth,
                                       Stirlingshire.
                                          N.B.
                       Sat.,29th.,Sept.,' 45.


Dear Mr. Smith,
              I have been asked by my husband
to write and tell you that your son is fit and well.
                He is being evacuated from Sumatra
and will be home soon.
              Yours sincerely,
```

On 1 October 1945 my parents received a letter from the Casualty Branch of the Air Ministry to the effect that I was now safe and in Allied hands. A copy of the letter is re-produced at Appendix B. This, together with the letter from Mrs Anderson above, brought to an end the uncertainty over my well- being that had existed since the telegram and letter received by them in March 1943. Only two years and three months!

Back to 16 September at Camp 3. It was a Sunday. We had a most notable visitor. It was Lady Edwina Mountbatten the Supremo's wife. She arrived that morning having flown from Singapore. She had visited Camp 2 and had now arrived at Camp 3. She was accompanied by Brigadier Lloyd, the Australian in charge of RAPWI, another Brigadier and Majors Lodge and Jacobs. Brigadier Lloyd gave an introductory speech which was followed by a speech by Lady Mountbatten. She then toured the camp and met all the POWs shaking hands with them. She asked me about my interpreting duties and my home circumstances. She then visited the sick bay and even the infectious diseases unit. One little 'tit bit' from her speech always sticks in my mind. She said, '*You boys will be pleased to know that when I left Singapore to come here, the Japanese General was hard at work with his boots off*'. She had a busy schedule, from here she was to fly to Palembang , then to Medan and back to Simpang Tiga where she was due to visit the women's camp at Bankinan. During her visit Wing Commander Davis told me that the plan was to move all the 'fit' POWs by barge down the River Siak on the 19th. On 16th eight hospital patients were flown out of camp and the following day things really started to happen. Firstly, eight POWs left by plane, then fifty, then thirty Australians and finally seventy British. Unfortunately the British had to return because of congestion at the airfield. By the end of the day three hundred and fifty POWs had been flown out. On the 18th all administration was handed over to the Dutch in anticipation of the departure of all the British POWs.

CHAPTER 7

Homeward bound

Mid-morning on 19 September turned out to be a day to remember. We received an urgent order to board three transport lorries which would take us to Camp 1 on the River Siak. Here we were to stay one night before onward transit, probably to Singapore. We arrived and had a brew of coffee. I then went to have a look at the timber built jetty on the river bank which had been built by the POWs. I had last been in Camp 1 on 28 May 1944 when there really wasn't a camp at all. Whilst on the jetty I looked to my right and round the bend in the river five vessels came into view. They were rather rusty but they were all flying the white ensign. Yes, they were all Royal Navy vessels. As they passed there was a shout from the loud hailer of the first vessel '*Which way to Pekanbaru?*' We indicated that it was straight on for about a quarter of a mile. They disappeared to our left but returned shortly afterwards. Two tied up to the jetty and the other three tied up alongside them. We were all instructed to return to camp where we were paraded, counted and then marched back to the jetty. The Naval Officers had a brief discussion with our Officers and then the Naval Officers divided us roughly equally between each vessel. When we boarded we were struck immediately by how fit and well the sailors looked when compared to the motley bunch of POWs who had just joined them. At this point I feel obliged to mention that the Dutch POWs who had been left behind weren't very happy (for obvious reasons). What they hadn't been told was that their presence may be required to suppress any Nationalistic uprising which was always a strong possibility. Once we were all aboard, the vessels 'cast-off' and sailed slowly down the river line astern leaving all our memories behind. Surely impossible! As we slowly followed the natural contours of the river my mind turned to a poem composed by a fellow POW at Kubang. I feel it says everything that we would all wish to say, especially the last verse.

Henry M Rees, MA
239 Battalion 77th HAA Regiment, RA

AT THE GOING DOWN OF THE SUN
To the south of Pekanbaru
Where the nightly tiger prowls
And the Simians greet the morning
With their ululating howls
Through the Kampong Katabalu
And the District of Kubang
There runs a single railway track
A monument to man.

In a short and fretful period
That was eighteen months of hell
Through the tangle of the tropics
And the oozing swamps as well
Through the cuttings that they hollowed

On embankments that they built
They have laid a modern railway line
On jungle trees and silt
And in spite of tropic noon-day
And a host of wasting ills
Ever southward went the railway
To Mauro in the hills
Every sleeper claimed a body
Every rail a dozen more
'twas the hand of fate that marked them
As it tallied up the score.

They could drag their aching bodies
To their grass and timber huts
They could rub the salt of impotence
In open weals and cuts
They could steel their will to conquer
To forget, perhaps forgive
But they found it mighty difficult
To force themselves to live.

When the day at last arrived
And when the rest of them were free
They devised a Union Jack and
They displayed it on a tree
And they thanked the God who made them
That he let them live again
And they prayed they might be better
For the suffering and the pain

There they left their friends behind them
Twenty times a score and more
Left them sleeping in the shadows

On a distant tropic shore
And I pray that God Almighty
In the evening of their lives
Will be gentle to their parents
And their children and their wives.

Progress down the river was slow and from time to time one of the vessels, despite being flat bottomed, would get stuck on a mud bank. One or two of the other craft would attach a hawser to the stricken vessel and tow it clear. We were told that they were Infantry Landing Craft (ILCs) and that they had sailed out East under their own steam. They were flat-bottomed meaning that the passage across open sea had been quite rough. Names had been painted on the front of the bridge. I recall three of them - Salerno, Messina and Palermo. It was explained that the vessels had played a very active part in landing Allied Invasion Forces at those locations. They had then travelled to Trincomalee in Ceylon in preparation for the planned invasion of Malaya and from there had been sent to assist in our repatriation.

It may seem silly and might well relate to the effect of freedom on the human psyche but, after some four years in the tropical environment, all the flowers, fauna and even the buildings suddenly became interesting and attractive even though they hadn't changed at all. The slow journey down the river was very relaxing and thoughts quickly turned to home and re-union with our loved ones. As darkness fell it was considered too risky to continue so we dropped anchor and all five vessels were roped together. Tying all the vessels together meant we were free to move between each one of them. I took this opportunity to catch up with old friends, particularly those from Camp 2. On one of the crafts a crew member was playing an accordion. We didn't recognise any of the tunes for the simple reason (as explained by the accordionist) that they had only been released whilst we were in captivity. This acted like a sort of advanced warning of how things had changed whilst we were in captivity and just how much we would have to adjust to get used to our newly found freedom. Spirits were high. Even a tropical downpour couldn't dampen them. As I was passing between crafts I bumped into Padre Rorke. He took me by the arm and, rather emotionally, said *'Smithy, there is something that I so much want to tell you. This is secret, but you are to be promoted back in the UK for your services as interpreter'*. I was taken aback. This came completely out of the blue but I am bound to confess that news like that is always welcome so I felt quite elated. For the record, nothing of the kind ever happened. In fact the UK Records Office was not even up to date with 1941 promotions (the records being lost) so instead of arriving back in the UK as Aircraftsman First Class I was recorded as Aircraftsman Second Class. The oversight was corrected once it was drawn to attention. I can only presume that Padre Rorke got his heavenly lines crossed!

Next morning we raised anchor and set sail down the river again. We eventually reached the point where the River Siak flows into open sea at the Malacca Straits. Here two large Tank Landing Craft were anchored. The original plan was that we were to board these craft as it was anticipated that the ILCs would have to return to collect more British POWs. However, the ILCs had managed to uplift all the British POWs so we remained on board and sailed down the Straits to

Singapore. After the calmness of the river, the sea swell was most noticeable and 'laid low' quite a few of the lads. We sailed on through the night and at 10.30 on the morning of 21 September 1945 arrived in Singapore Harbour. Here we received lots of NAAFI supplies.

We were taken by motor transport to the Alexandra Hospital. We were all admitted and had to be seen by the Hospital Medical Officer who was accompanied by our Camp 3 MO, Doc Braithwaite. He impressed me, as he gave a spontaneous medical history of each one of us to the Hospital MO. I felt 100% fit but Doc Braithwaite recalled that a couple of days before leaving Sumatra I had suffered a bout of renal colic and had been given a morphine injection. I suppose it was Doc Braithwaite's duty to disclose everything so that medical records were completely accurate. After this we were issued with clean pyjamas and our tattered prison clothing was taken away to be burnt. We showered and shaved and had a meal of good European food. We were told that we would all receive a complete new clothing issue shortly. The hospital beds were soft and springy so everything seemed like a dream, but there was always a nagging doubt that it might end. In the early hours of the 22nd I lay in my bed complete with mozzy net experiencing severe lower abdominal pain. I sent for the MO. He arrived, a big burly man wearing a type of Glengarry hat with two ribbons down the back. He was a Lieutenant Colonel. He gave me a thorough examination. It was the return of the colic so Doc Braithwaite was quite correct to mention it. The MO asked me where I came from. I said 'Penrith, Cumberland'. He told me he was from Orton Westmorland (some 20 miles from Penrith). Small world!

Each night we would retire to our beds and wake up next morning to find that eight to ten of the lads were missing. It turned out that they had been shipped out around 2am. Some had been flown to Colombo, Ceylon and others by sea to South Africa. Whilst I was at the hospital there was a party of Japanese soldiers working in the hospital grounds. One day I took the opportunity to speak to them. What a difference. They were now the prisoners. They were completely subservient in their attitude towards me which I could have exploited if I chose to. On the 29th there was a mass exodus of patients by ship. My group were not included as we were 'too fit' to meet the urgent criteria and, quite rightly, all available ships and planes were used to transport those patients requiring special hospital treatment.

On 5 October Nobby Clark and I were granted a four hour pass to go into Singapore. Having been in Singapore before we thought we knew our way around, but it had changed so much that we actually got lost. We eventually reached the city and decided to have a meal in a restaurant. I can't recall its name but inside we came across a POW who we had never seen since 10th Battalion Camp in Jakarta in late 1943. Back then the Kempetai brought into camp a badly beaten RA Englishman. His intriguing story goes as follows – At the capitulation of Java in March 1942 this guy chose to do a runner. He went into the jungle where he befriended a native Javanese girl and subsequently went through a form of marriage with her. Then by some devious means he obtained Portuguese Nationality and received all the relevant papers making him effectively a neutral. He and his wife then set up a fairly successful rope business. All was going well until he started an affair with a

Javanese hospital nurse. Later the nurse learnt that he was 'married' so promptly turned him in to the Kempetai. After being punished by the Kempetai he was returned to the POW camp and that was the last we saw of him until now. Here he was in the restaurant. He was sat talking to some white shirted, gold braided senior officers of the Occupation Forces who looked as if they were waiting to be served. As soon as he spotted us he came over to us before we could take a seat. He said *'I'm fed up of this stuffed shirt brigade, I'm going to tell them that you have brought me an urgent message and that I must excuse myself.'* He continued, saying that he had now taken on a new identity and from here on he was Inspector Stadden of the Singapore City Police. After talking briefly to the 'Officers' he re-joined us and we all left the restaurant together. We went across the road to a Chinese Restaurant and before entering he said *'I'll do the talking'*.

We had a lovely meal and he then confided in us that he didn't have any money and asked us how much we had? We both had a £5 note which all POWs had been given on arrival in Singapore. He said *'Leave it to me'* and called for the bill. This was duly presented to him and after a cursory glance at it he called for the manager. As soon as the manager arrived he complained most vociferously that the cost was far too high and added *'You are not dealing with the Japanese now you know. I am Inspector Stadden of Beach Road Police Station and will pay you what I think is a fair amount. Tomorrow, call and see me at the police station and we'll sort this matter out'*. With that we left. The manager was clearly unhappy and was still gesticulating towards us. Outside we jumped into a taxi and again he said *'Let me do the talking'*. He sat beside the driver and said to him *'Gasoline banyak susa'*. (Petrol will be difficult to obtain). The driver nodded and then our 'friend' struck again. *'If you call at Beach Road Police Station at 10 o'clock tomorrow I will let you have a supply of petrol coupons'*. As we reached our destination he talked to the driver and made motions as if to pay but the driver waved him away saying *'Oh no, I will call on you in the morning'* and with that drove off with a broad grin on his face. We then went to the New World Amusement Park where we had a drink and when it was time to leave our 'friend' took charge once again. He hailed one of the larger taxis which already contained three Australian soldiers. Jovially, he asked if we could share the taxi. They agreed and we all jumped in. During the journey he engaged the Aussies in conversation offering to make a contribution towards the fare. He ascertained their destination telling them that they had quite a long way to go and ours was 'just round the corner'. The taxi pulled up and our 'friend' gave them a small payment from our money. We alighted and the taxi drove off. Immediately, our friend started laughing out loud saying that their destination was *'in the next street'*. I am still ashamed that we allowed ourselves to be drawn into such company. We should have known better.

On 8 October we were moved from hospital to a transit camp at Meyer's Flats. This seemed to be the first real move towards repatriation. On arrival we each received a sealed envelope which contained a personal
Message from our King.
(Shown below)

BUCKINGHAM PALACE

The Queen and I bid you a very warm welcome home.

Through all the great trials and sufferings which you have undergone at the hands of the Japanese, you and your comrades have been constantly in our thoughts. We know from the accounts we have already received how heavy those sufferings have been. We know also that these have been endured by you with the highest courage.

We mourn with you the deaths of so many of your gallant comrades.

With all our hearts, we hope that your return from captivity will bring you and your families a full measure of happiness, which you may long enjoy together.

George R.I

September 1945.

Amongst all the euphoria of freedom and the impending journey home it was easy to forget all those that had been left behind. I met with Captain Armstrong who was able to give me details of the total number of deaths by nationality in camps as at 15 August 1945 –

Dutch	-	499
British	-	151

Australian	-	25
American	-	3
Indonesian	-	26
Norwegian	-	1
Unknown	-	1
Total	-	<u>706</u>

BUT between 15 August and 25 November 1945 there were a further 110 deaths bringing the total by nationality to –

Dutch	-	570
British	-	182
Australian	-	30
American	-	3
Indonesian	-	28
Norwegian	-	2
Unknown	-	1
Total	-	<u>816</u>

As at 15 September 1945 the RAPWI report to the South East Asia Command recorded the number of survivors on Sumatra as follows –

Dutch	-	3158
British	-	722
Australian	-	170
American	-	12
Danish	-	1
Norwegian	-	1
Indian	-	563
Total	-	<u>4627</u>

At this point we received details of the Japanese surrender in Singapore on 12 September 1945. The Allies were represented by Lord Louis Mountbatten and General William Slim, the Japanese by General Itagaki, Commander of the 7th Army, Malaya, Java and Sumatra (he deputised for Count Terauchi the Japanese Supreme Commander who was in hospital in Saigon with a stroke); Lieutenant General Numata, Chief of Staff to Terauchi; Lieutenant General Nakamura, Commander 18th Army, Siam; Lieutenant General Kimura, Commander of the Burma Army; Lieutenant Kinoshita, Commander 3rd Army HQ, Singapore; Vice Admiral Fukutomi, Commander 1st Southern Expeditionary Fleet, Singapore and Vice Admiral Shibata, Commander 2nd Southern Expeditionary Force, Surabaya.

Back at the Transit Camp at Meyer's Flats a large blackboard outside the Orderly Office displayed the names of the next draft of POWs to leave. I was included. I was to catch a ship the next day 9th October.

Next morning we paraded for roll call (not tenko any more) and then travelled by lorry to the harbour. Here we paraded again and another roll call was completed. I couldn't see any ships but there was an ILC tied to the jetty. One of the Senior NCOs was starting to get agitated and kept shouting *'Come on, come on, dress up in the rear rank. Pull your bloody socks up or you'll all miss the bloody boat'* It was none other than Company Sergeant Major Hunt (the one scared of the Jap guards). In the front rank was the Medical Orderly from Camp 3, Jock McAuley. I'm not sure if there was any previous between him and Hunt, but Jock 'snapped' and without warning stepped forward and grabbed Hunt by the shirt front and pushed him towards the water until he was leaning out over the side of the jetty. He threatened Hunt saying something like '*One more 'toot' out of you and you're in the bloody water*'. Most POWs saw Hunt as a coward (I had already had a run in with him) so Jock's actions were seen as justified and applauded by some of the lads. Hunt was completely deflated. We all boarded the ILC at 11.30am and travelled out into mid-harbour. At the same time a large passenger liner arrived and dropped anchor. The gangway stairs were lowered and we went alongside and climbed aboard. The ship was the MV Highland Monarch of the Royal Mail Line. She weighed 14,500 tons and was a welcome sight. She had travelled from Hong Kong and already had some POWs and Internees on board. We were allocated our accommodation which was on the forward mess deck. We sailed at 2pm and were told to expect a lifeboat drill and allocated a lifeboat station. Ours was E Deck boat station 4. Each boat was allocated a bosun (a member of the crew), an officer or NCO passenger and an equal mix of POWs and Internees both men and women. The drill got under way. We all donned lifejackets and lined up at our station. Our NCO was none other than CSM Hunt and one of our members was Jock McAuley. Hunt was busying himself and in typical fashion was trying to impress those female members present. Then he saw McAuley and his behaviour changed completely. He was more subdued and moderated his 'superior' attitude. I tried to envisage what would happen if we had to take to the lifeboat in earnest with this explosive mix!

Before leaving Singapore we were allowed to send a telegram indicating that we had been liberated and had reached Singapore. Please see Appendix B.

We sailed due west and reached Madras, India at around 7am on 14 October 1945. All the ships in the harbour 'hooted' their welcome to us. We were not allowed shore leave but the Regimental Band of the Oxford and Bucks Light Infantry came on board and entertained. They also provided the music for dancing in the evening but for me dancing was out as I was suffering from an inflamed left shin. We left Madras at 5pm on 15th heading for Colombo, Ceylon. On 16th I was admitted to the ship's hospital with perostitis (inflammation of the bone). I had first experienced this condition way back in July 1940 when I was at No 11 Technical Training School, Hereford. It never bothered me all the time in captivity so why it should return now is a mystery. We reached Colombo on the 17th and even though shore leave was allowed I couldn't participate as I was still laid up with my perostitis. We were allowed to send a telegram home again. On the 18th the battle cruiser HMS Nigeria entered the harbour and 'hooted' as it went alongside and that evening we had a visit from none other than Gracie Fields. She had come on board to give a concert but insisted on visiting the ship's hospital so I had the opportunity to meet her. She shook my hand and gave me her autograph and said *'Ee it's a grand feeling to be going home'*. She then left to give her concert saying *'Good night and God bless'*.

On the 24th we sailed into the Gulf of Aden. I was allowed to get up and go on deck. On the 25th we entered the Red Sea and the following day I was discharged from hospital as 'fit'. The rise in temperature was most noticeable. On the 27th we had an interesting experience. The Aircraft Carrier HMS Attacker came alongside and travelled at the same speed as us. Its crew were most interested to see if any of their relatives might be on board our ship. Names were passed to them but I'm not sure of any positive identification was made. They then signalled *'Best wishes for a safe and speedy return home after the harsh treatment at the hands of the Japanese. The Attacker hopes to be in the UK by 10 November'*.

The daily orders for the 28th were received and indicated that the following day we would arrive at Suez and would be going ashore in parties of 400 to receive winter uniform clothing. We would remain in Suez for two days. We then reduced speed significantly so as to reach Suez at the appointed time. Early in the morning of the 29th we arrived at Adabiya Military Docks near Port Tewfik and tied up. We were greeted by a number of senior officers and a military band was playing on the quayside. We then boarded transport and travelled to Ataka clothing depot where everyone was issued with a complete set of new clothing. In port we attended an Ensa Concert, had dancing in the First Class ballroom of the ship and went boating and bathing at Sandy Beach. Most enjoyable. Whilst in port we had a death on board. It was Sir Athol McGregor, the Chief Justice of Hong Kong. He was to be buried at sea. We left port at 8.15am and entered the Suez Canal at 9.15am sailing very slowly. We then entered the Great Bitter Lakes where we saw HMS Nelson and eventually reached Port Said at the northern end of the canal.

At 7.30am on 1 November the sea burial took place. A unique experience for me. The ship slowed down whilst the ceremony was conducted. On the 2nd we sailed passed the island of Crete and were told that we were expected to arrive in Southampton on 9 November. By now the ship's crew had changed from tropical whites to navy blue and in the afternoon of the 3rd we passed the islands of Sicily and Malta. We continued along the North African coast all the time the crew kept informing us of the various locations, Tunisia, Bizerta, the Island of Golita etc. At 6.30am on the 6th we sailed passed Gibraltar but didn't stop but a small vessel did join us to deliver some bags of mail. We continued northwards along the coasts of Spain and Portugal and entered the Bay of Biscay when the starboard engine stopped due to a fuel problem. The fault was soon resolved and we set sail again. We were told that the 9th would be our last day on board and that we should be arriving at Southampton at around 2pm. Early morning of the 9th found us off The Lizard, we saw the Eddystone Lighthouse blinking at us and by mid- morning were passing Portland Bill and shortly afterwards The Isle of Wight. A welcome sight. We took on a pilot and sailed up The Solent. We tied up at Atlantic Quay, Southampton at 2.20pm. A very strange feeling came over me. I felt that every single man on that ship would, over the past 3½ years, have never believed that we were ever going to see these shores again. Yet here we were back in England. For the first time in years we were required to form up in our respective Services. There were 38 RAF men, most of them my fellow POWs. We disembarked at 3.30pm. The band of the Royal Marines played 'God Save the King' and 'Land of Hope and Glory'. We went to one of the departure terminals where we received tea and cakes and the Post Office Telegraph Department was there to allow us to send a telegram home. See Appendix B.

From Southampton we went by train to Waterloo and the RAF Transit Hostel, The Ensleigh Hotel Gardens. That night I telephoned my former boss, Joseph Thompson to ask him to tell my parents that I had landed safely. The next day we travelled to the Reception Centre at Cosford where we were medically examined and interviewed by officers working on behalf of the War Crimes Commission who we presumed were looking for evidence of torture and mal-treatment. Then came a huge let down. We went into the stores hangar where a very junior WAAF had a large pair of scissors and was cutting off lengths of Campaign Medals and handing them to each of us. No ceremony here and a bitter disappointment after all we had been through. This completed all official matters so we were now free to leave. Those with less than 100 miles to travel could collect their leave and travel passes and leave immediately. Others, which included me, would travel on Sunday 11 November. The Transport Officer explained that the Sunday train service was much less frequent and in any case train timings were quite erratic. The next morning I caught the train and had a long wait at Preston for my connection as that train was already running 1¾ hours late. My train was due to arrive at Penrith at 6.30pm and my father, sister and a representative of the Royal British Legion had arrived at the station only to be told that the train was late and getting later. So they adjourned to the nearest hostelry and imbibed in a drink or two. The train eventually arrived at Penrith Station at 8.45pm. My mother was true to her word and stayed at home. We caught the taxi home. Here I was back in the town of my birth on the 11th day of the 11th month. Unbelievable!

I rang the door bell. My mother came to the door. She was 'full up' and couldn't speak. We embraced for what seemed an age never speaking a word. The saying 'actions speak louder than words' was most appropriate. I had come through the front door just as we had arranged, 'as if I was coming home from work' but I was only 1,616 days late, 1,294 of which had been spent in captivity.

We adjourned to the living room. The table had been set with a 'Welcome Home' cake in the centre and bows of red, white and blue ribbons tied at each corner. There were bottles of all kinds of drink many of which had been donated by neighbours and well-wishers. I was aware that my mother had hardly taken her eyes off me and was slowly coming to terms with having her son home. She eventually broke the silence and said '*Do you need a good wash son or is it sunburn?*' Typical of a mother. We had quite a few drinks and I unpacked my kit bags to reveal various souvenirs from my days in camp. One minute it was laughter and then tears. The celebrations continued and to their dying days my Mum and Dad steadfastly refused to admit that, for the first and only time in their lives, my sister and I had to put them to bed.

And so ends one man's war. Probably a lifetime's experiences crammed into four and a bit years. But was it worth it? I suppose it depends on your point of view. One thing I am sure about – it certainly brings out the best and worst in mankind!

Let me conclude by echoing the words of the great explorer Scott in his last letter from the South Pole in 1910 -

'I do not regret this journey, which has shown that Englishmen can endure hardships, help one another and meet death with as great a fortitude as ever.

W R Smith.

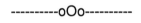

EPILOGUE

Penrith		Penrith Urban
Welcome Home		District Council
and		Town Hall
Appreciation		Penrith
Fund.		July 1946.

To Walter Raymond Smith

THE PEOPLE OF PENRITH send you this token of their appreciation of your service in the cause of freedom during the years 1939 to 1945, and on their behalf it is our pleasure to bring to you this fulfilment of what has truly been a wholehearted effort on the part of all Penrith people to welcome back into the life of the nation those who so readily went forth to battle for its preservation. By attaching their Common Seal the Council show that the Town of Penrith is officially identified with the Welcome Home Committee in this expression of appreciation and we all hope that you have now resumed or will soon come back to that normal life which was interrupted by War Service.

Yours very truly,

L. HARKER, Chairman of the Council.
J. E. IRVING, Chairman of the Welcome Home Committee.
C. H. HUNTLEY, Clerk of the Council and Hon. Secretary of the Fund.
WM. BROWN, Hon. Treasurer of the Fund.

In July 1946 all returning members of the Armed Forces received a letter (above) from the Welcome Home Fund and Penrith Urban District Council.

At the end of the war the Armed Forces provided a series of re-settlement schemes aimed at providing training in both academic and practical skills for returning service personnel. Successful candidates could either remain in the Forces or apply their newly acquired skills elsewhere. It was logical for me to try and make use of my Japanese language skills and, perhaps, obtain employment in post-war Japan. Following normal leave, repatriation leave, foreign- service leave and unexpired normal leave I was recalled to 115 RAF Re-settlement Centre at Sunninghill Park in Berkshire on 12 February 1946. I eventually attended the School of Oriental Studies at London University where I took an oral exam in the Japanese language. I was interviewed by Professor Daniells and an un-named Japanese. I felt that, without being exceptional, I answered all their questions. After a wait of three weeks I was called to see Squadron Leader Boycott at the Unit Orderly Office. He read me the letter from the university. It said I had 'passed' the exam but my grammar was unsound and, even though they offered me a place at the university, it would require a lot of work on my part to reach the standard of existing students. Because of this I abandoned the idea immediately.

My accumulated leave continued to 25 August 1946 after which I commenced my civilian employment.

The reader may recall that on 1 September 1945, Captain Armstrong and I agreed to give Sergeant Major Ebinuma a letter of 'safe conduct' in recognition of his compassionate nature and kindness shown to the POWs in Camp 3.

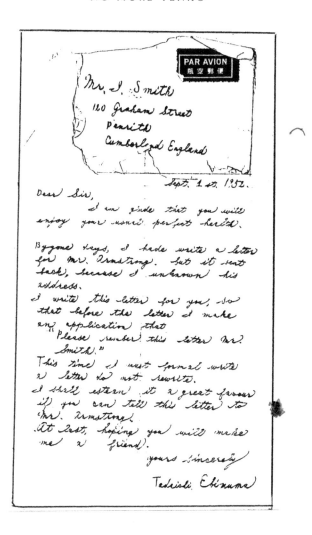

In September 1952 I received a letter of thanks from Ebinuma (It is dated 1 September 1952) exactly seven years later). At the time I didn't feel disposed to reply. Perhaps I should have done. The letter is shown above.

Akama, Simotuga-gun,
Totigi Prefecture,
Japan, Aug. 21 st. 1952.

My dear sir,

It is quite an age since I wrote to you last.
How have you been keeping? We are all
firstrate.

As you know, our Crown Prince went over to
your country to attend the glorious Coronation
Ceremony as proxy of the Emperor. We Japanese
are all rejoiced to hear that he was heartily
welcomed in all parts of your country.

I was disgorged through your kindness and
are now spending a peaceful life playing
an active part in many ways. I hold a
responsible post in our village. Our agricultural management has been started in a
right direction.

We have had too much rain this summer and
flood damages struck several parts of our
country, and now we are having an unbearably
hot weather.

I think, in your country, summer is rather
bearable compared with that of Japan.

Please take great care of yourself.
Send my best wishes to Mr. Smith.
My Christian name, Tadaiti, is said
to be a very good name, which means
"only one" in English. "Tada" is the Japanese for "only" and "iti" is for "one".
"Tadaiti" means "unparalleled" or
"unique".
Please write as soon as possible.

Truly yours,

Tadaiti Ebinuma.

In August 1952 Ebinuma had written to Captain Armstrong directly (shown above). This letter was also not replied to and in fact both letter were mislaid until October 1988 when they re-surfaced.

In 1988 I decided to try and trace Ebinuma through the Japanese Red Cross Society in Tokyo. I learnt that he had died in December 1979 at the age of 76. They did provide me with the name and address of his daughter Yoshiko Shimamura who owned a restaurant in Fujiyoka. Consequently, we wrote to each other regularly and in 1994 my daughter visited Japan where she was very warmly received by Mrs Shimamura, her brothers (Ebinuma's sons) and her immediate family who seemed to acknowledge that it was the actions of her father (me) that prevented their father from being executed as a war criminal.

APPENDIX A

The Pekanbaru to Muaro Railway

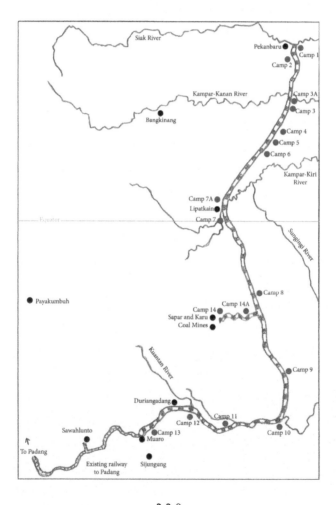

Camp No	Camp Name	Opened
1	Pekanbaru	24.5.44
2	Tangkirang	24.5.44
3	Kotabulu	June 44
3A	Kobang	26.11.44
4	Kampar Kanan	July 44
5	Lubuk Sakat	July 44
6	Singai Pagar	Oct 44
7A	Kampar Kiri	22.4.45
7B	Lipatkain	Dec 44
8	Kota Baru	May 45
9	Logas	Jun 45
10	Lubuk	Jul 45
11	Padang Torok	10.8.45
12	Silukah	12.7.45
13	Muaro	7.3.45
14	Tappei	
14A	Petai	

APPENDIX B

Letters, telegrams and newspaper articles

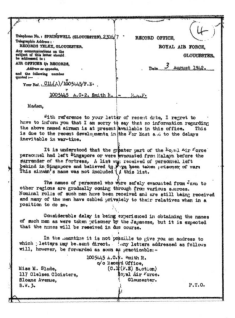

Telephone No. : SPRINGWELL (GLOUCESTER) 2306/7
Telegraphic Address :
RECORDS TELEX, GLOUCESTER.
Any communications on the
subject of this letter should
be addressed to :
AIR OFFICER i/c RECORDS,
Address as opposite,
and the following number
quoted :—

Your Ref. : OLL(A)/1005445/P.E.

RECORD OFFICE,

ROYAL AIR FORCE,

GLOUCESTER.

Date 3 August 1942.

1005445 A.C.2. Smith R. R.A.F.

Madam,

With reference to your letter of recent date, I regret to
have to inform you that I am sorry to say that no information regarding
the above named airman is at present available in this office. This
is due to the recent developments in the Far East and to the delays
inevitable in war-time.

It is understood that the greater part of the Royal Air Force
personnel had left Singapore or were evacuated from Malaya before the
surrender of the fortress. A list was received of personnel left
behind in Singapore and believed to have been taken prisoner of war.
This airman's name was not included in this list.

The names of personnel who were safely evacuated from Java to
other regions are gradually coming through from various sources.
Nominal rolls of such men have been received and are still being received
and many of the men have cabled privately to their relatives when in a
position to do so.

Considerable delay is being experienced in obtaining the names
of such men as were taken prisoner by the Japanese, but it is expected
that the names will be received in due course.

In the meantime it is not possible to give you an address to
which letters may be sent direct. Any letters addressed as follows
will, however, be forwarded as soon as practicable:-

1005445 A.C.2. Smith R.
c/o Record Office,
(O.L1(P.E) Section)
Royal Air Force.
Gloucester.

Miss M. Slade,
117 Chelsea Cloisters,
Sloane Avenue,
S.W.3.

P.T.O.

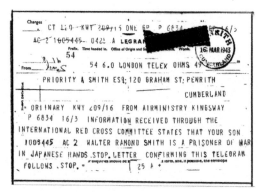

Charges

CT 129 -- KWY 209/15 ONE GP P 6834
AC-2 1005445- 0425 A LEGRAM
54
From
54 6.0 LONDON TELEX OHMS 49

16 MAR 1943

PRIORITY A SMITH ESQ; 120 GRAHAM ST; PENRITH

CUMBERLAND

ORDINARY KWY 209/16 FROM AIRMINISTRY KINGSWAY
P 6834 16/3 INFORMATION RECEIVED THROUGH THE
INTERNATIONAL RED CROSS COMMITTEE STATES THAT YOUR SON
1005445 AC 2 WALTER RAMOND SMITH IS A PRISONER OF WAR
IN JAPANESE HANDS .STOP. LETTER CONFIRMING THIS TELEGRAM
FOLLOWS .STOP. 25 A

NO MORE TENKO

231

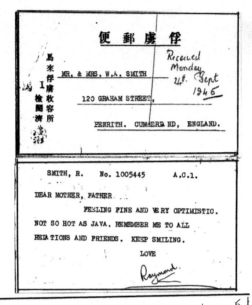

便郵虜俘

馬
來
伖
虜
牧
容
所
I
檢
閲
濟

MR. & MRS. W.A. SMITH

120 GRAHAM STREET,

PENRITH. CUMBERLAND, ENGLAND.

Received Monday 24th Sept 1945

SMITH, R.   No. 1005445   A.C.1.

DEAR MOTHER, FATHER

FEELING FINE AND VERY OPTIMISTIC.

NOT SO HOT AS JAVA. REMEMBER ME TO ALL

RELATIONS AND FRIENDS. KEEP SMILING.

LOVE

Raymond.

Received Oct 1st 1945

Telephone Gerrard 9234
Extn.
Any communications on the
subject of this letter
should be addressed to:-
THE UNDER SECRETARY OF
STATE.
and the following number
quoted:-
P401348/43/P4PW/B.5
Your Ref.

AIR MINISTRY

(Casualty Branch)

73 - 77 OXFORD STREET,

W.1.

29.9.45

Sir/~~Madam~~

I am directed to state that information has been received
that *1005445. AC2. W.R. SMITH.*
is safe in Allied hands.

Although it may be some time before he arrives in the United
Kingdom you will doubtless hear from him direct before long.
In any case, information of a general character regarding
recovered prisoners, including their movements before they
reach home, will be given from time to time on the wireless and
will be published in the press.

I am, Sir/~~Madam~~
Your obedient Servant,

(Hand.a.

W.A. Smith. Esq.

RECOVERED PRISONERS OF WAR
ON ACTIVE SERVICE
BY AIR MAIL

ADDRESS ONLY

POSTAGE
FREE

Received Oct 17. 1945

To
MR AND MRS W.A. SMITH,
120 GRAHAM STREET,
PENRITH, CUMBERLAND
ENGLAND.

My address is
C/o GREEN RECEPTION CENTRE
INDIA

DEAR Mum + Dad.

I am now free and in safe hands.

I hope to be with you soon

Signature WRSmith

Date 8 · 10 · 45

C.Pt.C./PSS/2744/7-45/20000.

Printed in England.   Sept 1943
(11,000 Pads.)   (1,400 Bmks.)

CABLE AND WIRELESS
LIMITED
"Via Imperial"

The first line of this Telegram contains the following particulars in the order named
Prefix Letters and Number of Message. Office of Origin. Number of Words. Date. Time handed in.
Official Instructions—if any.

19 OCT.1945

Circuit.   Clerk's Name.   Time Received.

X 58346

C W   WSA   1636/U   COLOMBO   18OCT

FWM   MR   AND   MRS   W   A   SMITH

120   GRAHAM   STREET   PENRITH   CUMBERLAND   =

ARRIVED   SAFELY   AT   COLOMBO   *   HOPE   BE

HOME   SOON   *   WRITING   *   ADDRESS   LETTERS   AND

TELEGRAMS   TO   CARE   PO   BOX   164   LONDONEC1   =

R   SMITH   *

Extracts from the "Cumberland
& Westmorland Herald"

16th March 1943.

After a period of anxiety extending over fourteen months two Penrith families received information through the Red Cross which to some extent relieves their fears. Mr. and Mrs. W. A. Smith, Graham Street, Penrith, have had a letter stating that their only son, Aircraftman Walter Raymond Smith, R.A.F., who fourteen months ago was posted missing when Malaya was over-run, is now reported to be a prisoner of war in the hands of the Japanese. There is no intimation as to where he is situated. Before the war Aircraftman Smith was employed by Messrs. G. and J. Thompson, the Penrith engineers, with whom his father is secretary.

1st January 1944.

LOCAL WAR CASUALTIES

NEWS OF PENRITH PRISONERS

Postcards have been received this week from three Penrith prisoners in Japanese hands.

Although she had previously been informed by the Red Cross Society that he was a prisoner in Japanese hands, Mrs. Faulder, Tyne Close Avenue, has this week received the first communication for two years from her husband, Leading Aircraftman W. A. Faulder. He states that he is a prisoner in a Java camp and is all right. L.A.C. Faulder, who is a flight mechanic, is a son of Mr. and Mrs. Alf. Faulder, Castle Drive.

Yesterday morning, Mr. W. A. Smith, Graham Street, received the first communication which he has had from his son, Aircraftman Ronald Smith, for two years. Ronald was in Malaya with Aircraftman Faulder, and his parents were aware that he was a prisoner. He states that he is all right and that the Japanese are treating them well.

8th July 1944.

PENRITH PRISONER IN JAVA

Mr. and Mrs. W. A. Smith, Graham Street, Penrith, on Wednesday received a postcard from their son, Aircraftman W. Raymond Smith, R.A.F., who was taken prisoner when the Japanese occupied Java in March, 1942. They were not informed of this through the Red Cross until a year later, and it was not until 31st Dec., 1943, that they received the first postcard from him. The postcard which came on Wednesday is dated 3rd November, 1943, and its message indicates that Aircraftman Smith is quite well. He has been in the R.A.F. since July, 1940, and went to the Far East in August, 1941.

PROLONGED CRUELTY AT SINGAPORE

MORE EVIDENCE

FROM OUR SPECIAL CORRESPONDENT

SINGAPORE, SEPT. 13

One unfortunate result of the unavoidable delay in reoccupying South-East Asia is that the Japanese have had plenty of time to destroy incriminating evidence. The *Kempeitai* have burned nearly all their records.

But certain documents have escaped destruction, and General Mansergh yesterday showed correspondents some revolting photographs, undoubtedly genuine, which had been found on top of a cupboard in a Japanese headquarters where all other documents had been destroyed. The first photograph showed Indians, whether soldiers or civilians it was difficult to say, but they were probably the latter, loaded in trucks. The second showed them blindfolded and sitting waiting to be shot in a shooting range, with a piece of dark cloth pinned over their hearts as bulls' eyes. The third showed the Japanese soldiers firing at them at a range of about 300 yards, a distance at which they were unlikely to secure a direct hit. A spurt of dust in the hillside behind the prisoners confirmed that not all bullets found their mark.

The fourth showed the Japanese soldiers bayoneting the Indians, who quite obviously were still alive, having survived the target practice. The fifth showed a group of Indian girls and children weeping, one seemed to have fainted, suggesting the families of these Indians had been made to witness the spectacle.

In one way, this return to Singapore has been very depressing. Every day grisly stories are coming out, so well authenticated that there can be no doubting them. A special organization is investigating the atrocities, and officers of it gave details of certain of the cases this evening. In one case, which occurred before the capitulation, from 110 Australians captured up country, including many wounded, only three survived. The Japanese maltreated them with every conceivable brutality. After mowing many down with machine-guns they poured petrol on the remainder and set fire to them.

AMUCK IN HOSPITAL

During fighting on the island, Japanese troops ran amuck in the Alexandra Hospital and as well as killing many patients and the hospital staff, they bayoneted one patient who was undergoing an operation on the operating table. In September 42 senior British officers at Changi and various allied commanders of prison camps were forced to see the shooting of two British and two Australians charged with trying to escape. One took all the blame and begged that he alone should be killed. All, when offered handkerchiefs, scornfully refused. The Japanese shooting was wild, and one man cried out, " For God's sake shoot me. You have only hit me in the arm." The Japanese continued firing until all were dead. From one party of 7,000 men, British and Australians, including 2,000 sick, sent north in May, 1942, to work on the worst section of the Moulmein-Bangkok railway, 3,000 were dead by December.

The Japanese provided no dressings for tropical ulcers, and the men had to work with shinbone bared from knee to ankle or covered only with camp dressings of puttees and banana leaves. From 75 amputations only two survived. The tale of horror is endless. And for every European who died on the railway there were 20 among conscripted Indian, Chinese, and Burmese coolies. For every brutality against Europeans in Singapore, there were 100 against the local people, especially the Chinese.

'LIVING DEAD' RAIL SLAVES

A story of war prisoner slave labour exceeding in callousness that of the building of the Bangkok-Moulmein railway is expected to come out of Sumatra, says Alan Humphreys, Reuter's correspondent in Singapore.

News of Japanese brutality towards British, Australian and Dutch war prisoners set to work on building the central Sumatra railway was radioed from Sumatra by South African Major Jacobs, a member of "Mastiff Organisation" which deals with air supplies of medical requirements, food and clothing for released prisoners.

First to be dropped by parachute into Sumatra, Maj. Jacobs has been visiting war prisoner and internee camps, flying in a Japanese plane, piloted by a Japanese.

He described as "living dead" those who had worked on railway.

Maj. Jacobs also reported shocking conditions and appalling atrocities at Rantauparaput camp, accommodating 6,000 internees, including 500 British women and children, and said that at the Allied POW camp at Palembang 249 died in three months from illness and malnutrition.

A fatigue party made up of Jap POW's is shown on hands and knees cleaning up in Singapore. Most of the territories reoccupied by Allied forces have been found in dirty and neglected condition and the Jap prisoners were immediately put to work straightening the situation.

APPENDIX C

The War Graves
in Menteng Pulu, Java

(With apologies for the quality – the originals have been mislaid)

The War Graves Plaque

L C J Heard died 25.7.45 (*See Page 173*)

G G Carrington died 5.9.45 (*See Page 186*)

W Vallance died 29.8.45 (*See Page 184*)

AE Rouse died 16.7.45 (*See Page 173*)

W A Smith died 9.8.45 (*See Page 173*)

A Moore died 20.8.45 (*See Page 173*)

A E A Wales died 15.4.45 (*See Page 171*)

J Stevenson died 9.7.45 (*See Page 172*)

APPENDIX D

The Author – Walter Raymond Smith

Photograph taken at Kuala Lumpur,
Malaya on 21 September 1941

NAMES INDEX

Nationality code - A = American AUS = Australian B = British
C = Chinese D = Dutch
(in brackets) I = Irish J = Japanese K = Korean
NZ = New Zealand SA = South African

ACKNOWLEDGEMENTS

To the Author's daughters Susan and Judith and son Peter for their support and encouragement. Also for providing additional material which proved invaluable.

To my partner Christine for her patience and understanding, particularly in the early stages of the project when I went missing for hours on end.

To Steve Buck at the Cumberland and Westmorland Herald Office in Penrith for his advice on technical issues and help with printing the early drafts.

To Victoria Reay for creating and producing the front cover illustration.

To my friends Bob Parker and Eric Hall for taking the time to read my early draft and for their honest feedback.

Finally, to my late father in law who gave me the inspiration to embark on this project. His meticulous record keeping and attention to detail and the amount of information readily to hand convinced me that the project was worth pursuing. I have taken great care not to compromise or alter his intended message and only hope that I have succeeded. He deserves no less.

J Walker
Co-Author